Practical Boat Bits and Tips

The simplest and best ideas compiled from building, maintaining, and managing small vessels for forty years.

Illustrated with photographs and diagrams, and in Jude's unique style.

As Cap'n Jack says, "The best advice; she keeps *Banyandah* in top shape."

Judith Binder has more than forty years experience finishing and maintaining vessels, furniture, and houses. She is an accomplished sailor with 150,000 miles under sail, so she knows what stands the test of time. She learnt how to organize, victual, and manage a ship by living continuously afloat for sixteen years while raising and educating her two sons and sailing to over eighty countries.

In 2007, Jack and Jude, then married forty years and grandparents to five devishingly cute grandchildren, circumnavigated Australia aboard their beloved *Banyandah*.

After that they wrote the inspirational book, "Two's a Crew"

Six years ago Jack and I completed a full refit of *Banyandah* inside and out, from the bottom of her keel to the top of her mast. Although she was a near perfect cruiser, she'd sailed more than one hundred thousand nautical miles housing a family with two sons fully educated aboard her, and she was worn out from all the work. Coupled with what we'd learnt over those years, this refit gave us the opportunity to correct inherent faults. So we gutted our baby. Ripped it all out. Took a sandblasting hose inside, and then started again with a bare hull. Since then, another chunk of sea miles has passed under her keel and once again she's proved a very workable ship.

Keep it Simple

For Safe and Comfortable Cruising

This book is for all with the desire to enjoy life afloat. It is not about what you need to go 'cruising'. There are plenty of those books already written. This is a pictorial view, with notes on how we've set up *Banyandah*, and some practical bits and tips that have helped make *Banyandah* a pleasure to sail and life a little bit easier. After all sailing is often hard work.

To the men wanting to take their ladies sailing – keep it simple – and don't shout too much, and never in anger – words can be blown away with the wind or misheard. Deck work; in particular when raising the anchor can mostly be done by using clear hand signals.

And to the crew – remember A Crew must work with each other – only one can be in command.

Practical Boat Bits and Tips

Jude Binder

Thanks Jack for your patience.

All photographs and diagrams by Judith and Jack Binder

First published in Australia 2011

Second edition Worldwide 2020

Tujays Publishing
Empire Vale P.O., NSW
Australia 2478
Email: capjack2j@gmail.com
Web: www.jackandjude.com

Papers used in the production of this book are natural, renewable and recyclable products sourced from sustainable forests and certified in accordance with the rules of Forest Stewardship Council, PEFC & FSC.

Note: Both imperial and metric measurements used throughout.
1 nautical mile (NM) = 1.15 land miles (m) = 1.852 kilometres (km)
Australian dollars are shown
Australian spelling is used

National Library of Australia
Cataloguing-in-Publication entry:
Binder, Judith, 1945 - .
Practical boat bits and tips / writing by Judith Binder;
photographs by Jack Binder & Judith Binder.
ISBN: 9780980872040 (pbk.)
1. Boats and boating--Handbooks, manuals, etc

797.1

Table of Contents

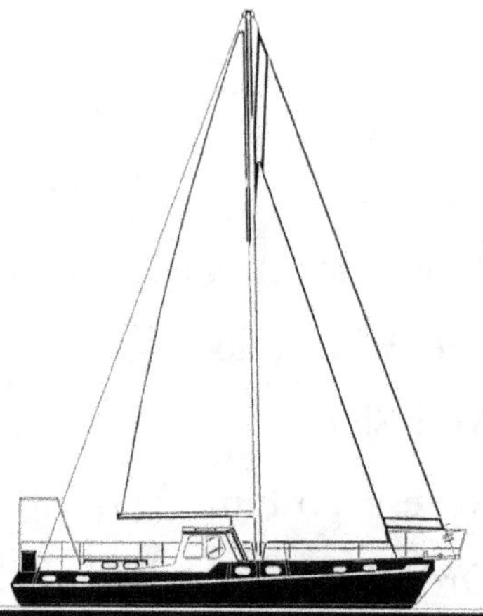

Practical Boat Bits and Tips

Sailing coastal or offshore you'll surely want your boat, nuisance free and easy to manage, as well as ship shape. Attention to detail helps make cruising life a pleasure. We like to sail along and do things aboard without fuss, and the ability to fix things ourselves is simply a great asset.

So keep the boat simple. Avoid unnecessary gadgets, get manuals when you can and learn how to fix things yourself. That way you won't be searching for a secure berth in a marina for someone to fix it for you.

In this book I have put together some ideas that we find useful and quick fix solutions. Some won't be right for your boat, but they might spawn an idea that will be.

Being afloat requires thought and planning, and diligence to detail, and being responsible to take care of yourselves.

To us it's a job. Always working, everyday; in love with a boat; waking through the night to the wind, feeling how she's reacting.

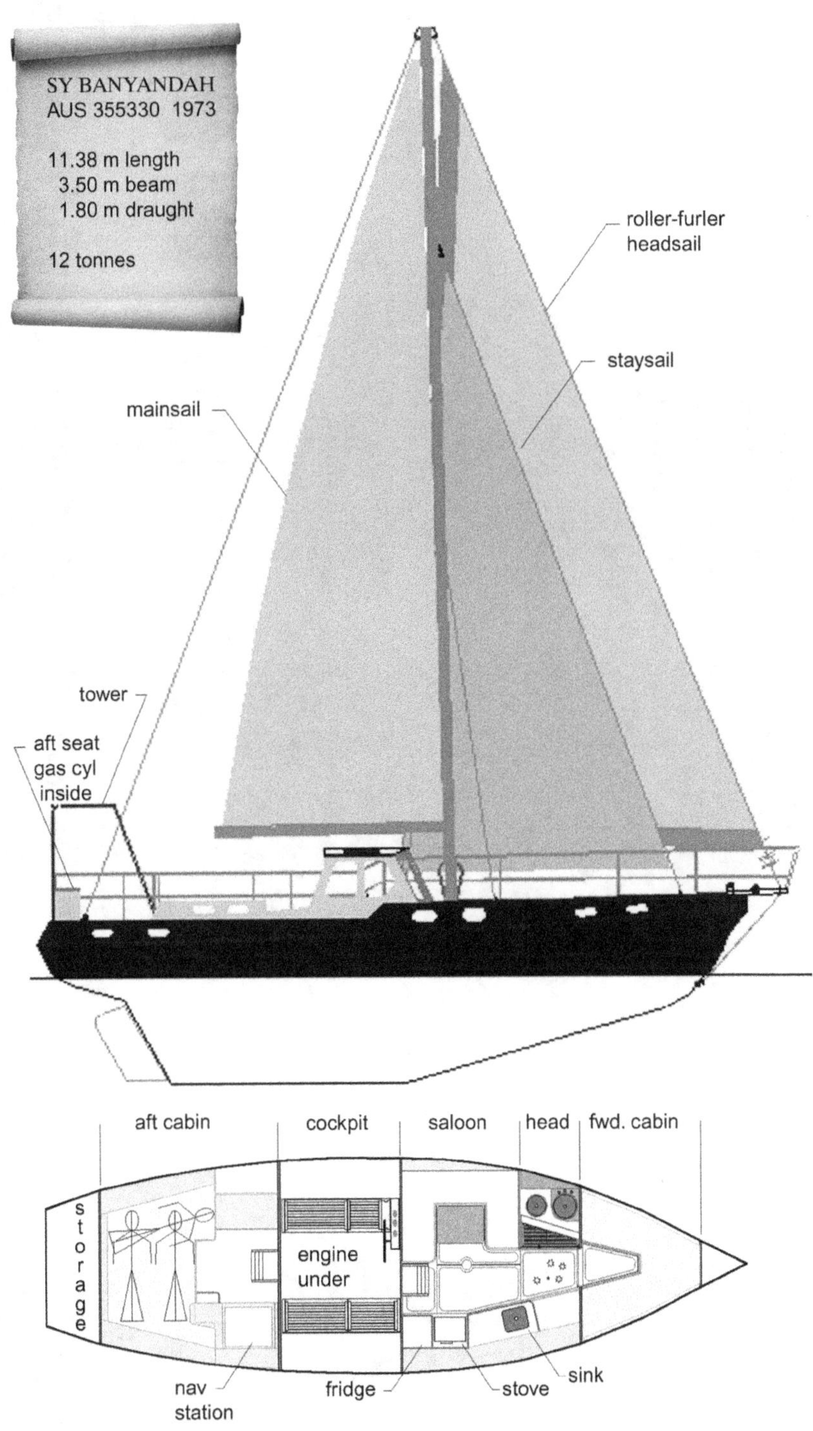
SY BANYANDAH
AUS 355330 1973
11.38 m length
3.50 m beam
1.80 m draught
12 tonnes
roller-furler
headsail
staysail
mainsail
tower
aft seat
gas cyl
inside
aft cabin
cockpit
saloon
head
fwd. cabin
storage
engine
under
sink
nav
station
fridge
stove

Welcome Aboard Banyandah

Welcome aboard *Banyandah.*

I hope by perusing this book some helpful ideas to fix tricky situations will show up or spawn a solution for you.

Looking Forward

On this centre cockpit yacht the saloon is to port, then the head, then the forward cabin. To starboard is the gimballed stove and out of sight further aft is the top opening fridge.

Handholds in the frames of our flush deck cutter occur throughout the boat.

Above the galley is a hatch.

In moderate conditions at sea, this hatch is sometimes left ajar for ventilation

The dinghy sits over it and provides some protection from any sea slop that might sneak aboard.

The bottom door below the two drawers in the galley drops down as does the door under the stove.

Note stainless steel saddle for galley strap just to left of stove door.

Use a Noodle

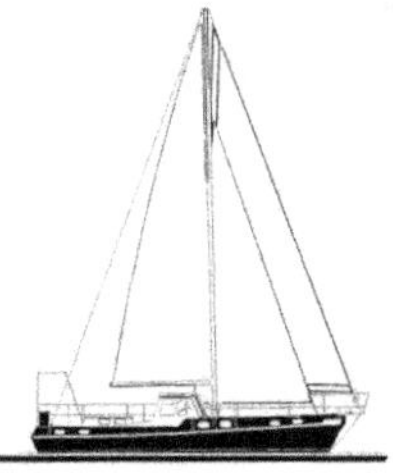

Get rid of those annoying rattles and clunks.

Apart from being a great toy for the kids in the pool or as an aid for swimming lessons, there are many good places to use pool noodles.

This piece silences chatter when the two stays are pulled together when the awning is up.

Size 70 mm.

Cut it quickly with a breadknife.

It's not necessary to cut it exactly to size.

The noodle compresses so can be pressed into the space.

Noodles in the Galley

Cup and Mug Storage

70 mm size noodle fits most cups, mugs and glasses.

Position mugs on the shelf.

Mark around the outside leaving enough space for the handles.

Cut 30 mm slices. Centre and glue down with contact.

This top opening cupboard is behind the galley.

The gas turn off in the galley is within easy reach behind the stove. The gutter around the top opening cupboard – it drains spills back onto the galley and not down into the cupboard.

More Noodles
Tall Bottle Storage

Part of the galley cupboard under the sink has been sectioned off with 12 mm x 100 mm wood. The spaces are large to accommodate a variety of shapes or sizes.

The noodle fills the gap and keeps bottles upright. Used either way, flat or round against the bottles, they stay upright.

I prefer oil in glass bottles. However, once when leaving the Mediterranean after being in Italy we had on board some Extra Virgin Olive Oil that our dear friend Geppino had suggested. One nearly full bottle got away at sea and fell to the cabin sole.

Need I say more! But, oil is safe in glass bottles, but for safety I keep mine upright in the breakfast locker protected by a sock muff.

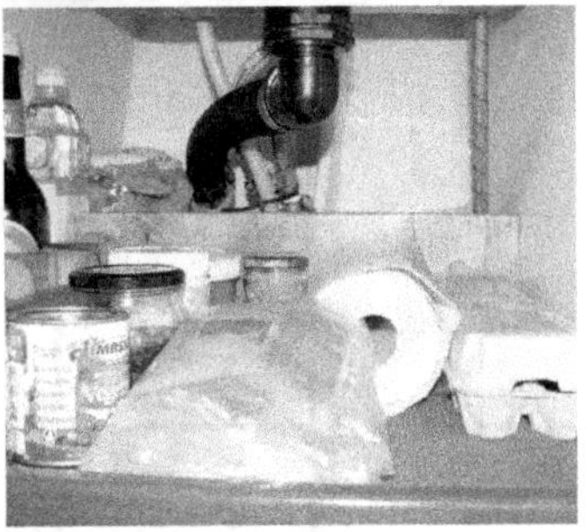

Low fiddle at back of cupboard keeps everyday food in reach.

More than Noodles

This small locker behind the saloon is very handy for special tots! The cupboard front has a deep fiddle.

A grid of 100 mm x 3 mm plywood has been glued together to fit into the cupboard.

Thin pieces of pool noodle bend easily and hold the bottles in place.

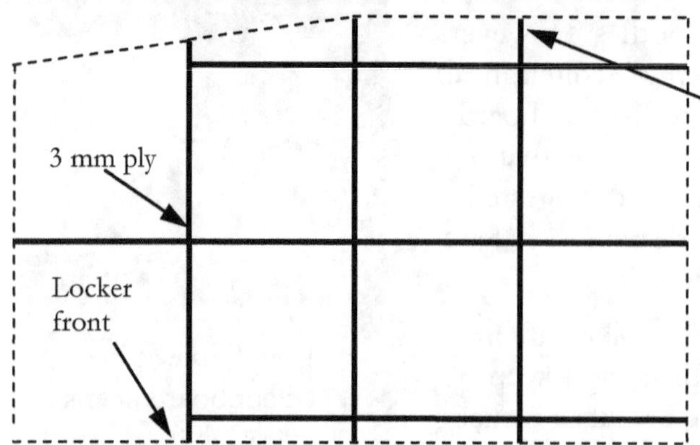

The ply was left long at the back then shaped to fit snugly afterwards.

Tip. Vary the grid size to accommodate a few larger bottles.

Noodles in Drawers

You need a cupboard that is easy to get in and out of at sea in all conditions. This galley drawer suits me. I can take the lids off a container and leave the jar where it is, it can't fall, or I can put something down on the noodle between them. Supported by my galley strap I have hands free, and a knee rested against the drawer keeps it open. At odd times I have wondered how a lock would go to keep it open while in use at sea.

The noodle at the back is split lengthways and fits firmly against the sides. All noodles are cut slightly long. They work best pressed into place. The timber baffles are held in place by the noodles so the entire drawer can be changed when I want to. And everything comes out for easy cleaning.

Tip. All drawers should have a secure locking system. We use recessed slide bolts on all drawers but also have a secondary backup just in case. This is made from cord.

Braided Cord Restrainer for Drawers

Prevent drawers accidentally flying out.

Drill two holes, one each side in the back of the drawer.

Tie a knot in one end of the cord and slip the other end through the hole from inside.

Take it round a strong point behind the drawer and come back through the opposite hole.

The cord needs to be of sufficient length to be able to do this while the drawer is out.

Replace the drawer, and then adjust how far you want it to come out.

Pull on the cord until you have taken out all the slack while the drawer is in that position and tie a knot in the end.

> ***Tip.*** Make the knots big enough so they won't pull back through the hole.
>
> The drawer back needs to be well attached.

Noodle in the Head

Stabilize the plumbing against the hull.

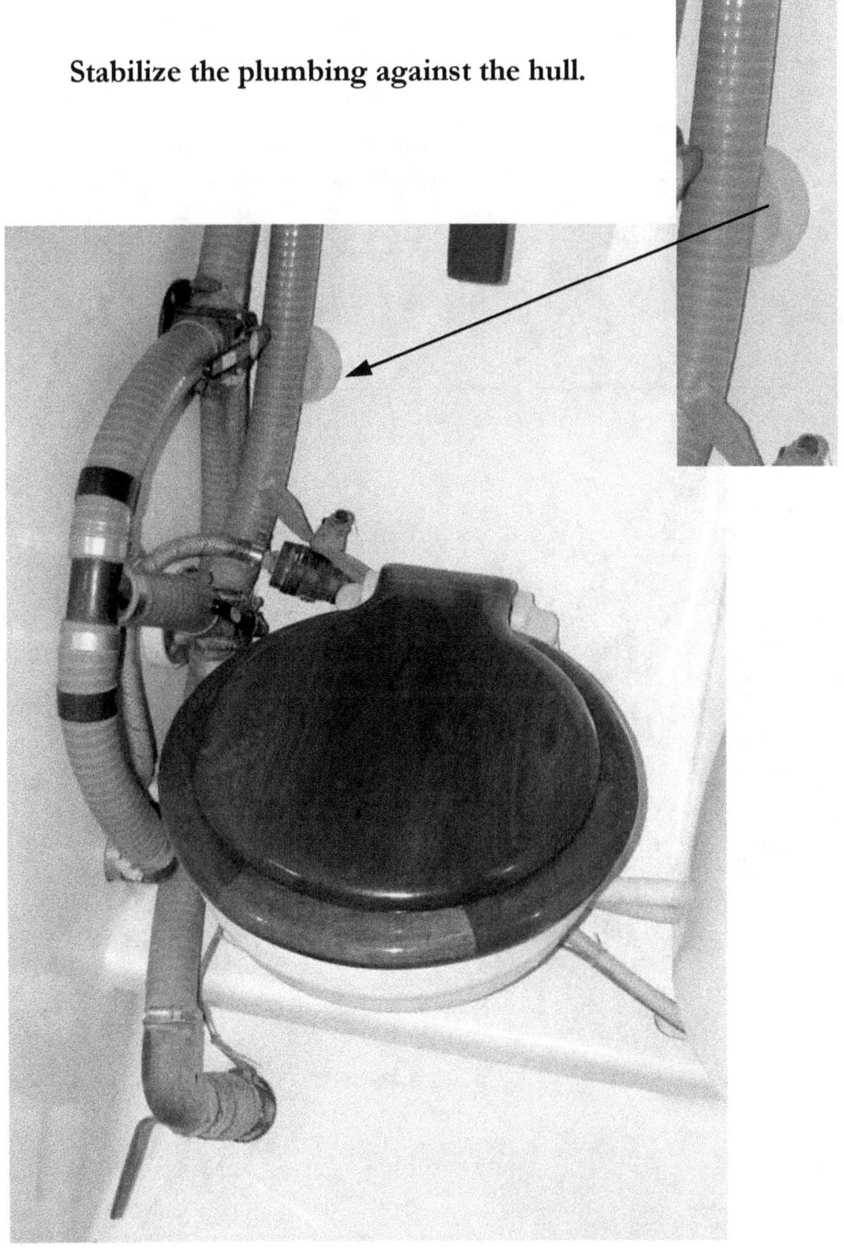

To Help the Noodle

The (red) ribbon on the seawater intake valve is a reminder to turn it off after use.

It is useful, all the more so when visitors are on board.

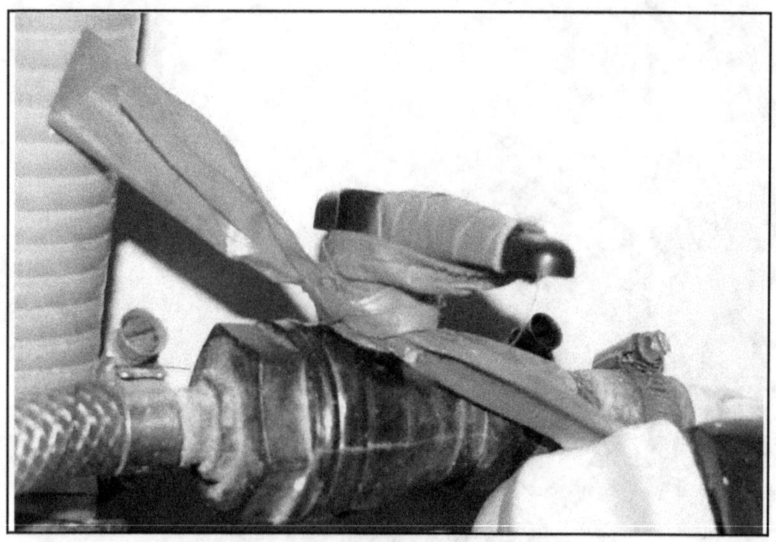

Anti-Skid

Instead of non-skid tape these treads have been sanded. I find this better than anti-skid tape.

Sand on Steps

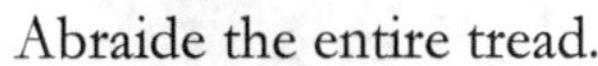

Abraide the entire tread.

Mask around the area to be made anti-skid.

Varnish the masked area then sprinkle heavily with blasting sand.

Allow to dry 24 hrs.

Remove tape and brush away loose sand.

Completely varnish over the whole tread stippling well into sanded area.

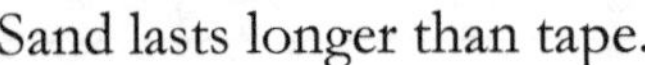

Sand lasts longer than tape.

Tip. Pour a small amount of varnish into a can or container to use, so as not to contaminate the good stuff with sand.

Anti-Skid on the Cabin Sole

The cabin sole is sealed with single pack satin varnish and is fairly non-skid as is.

Areas where the floor is likely to get wet, (outside the head and near the galley) have had shapes cut out the cork and filled with Sikaflex. Sanded flat they give good foothold.

Do not varnish.

6 mm cork laid on 12 mm structural grade ply with type A waterproof bond. It is lightweight and easy to lift up.

The floor reaches right to the cupboard fronts so it gives great exposure to the bilge area.

Tip. Cork and plywood flooring is economical.

Access to Hull and Fittings

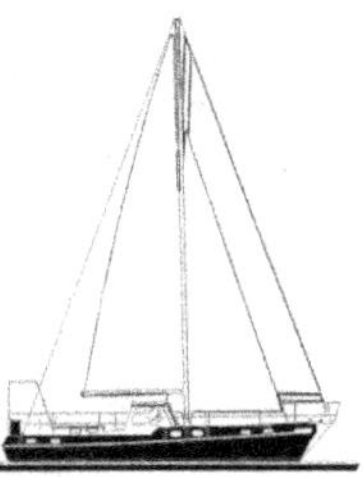

Galley floor standing on edge gives good exposure below.

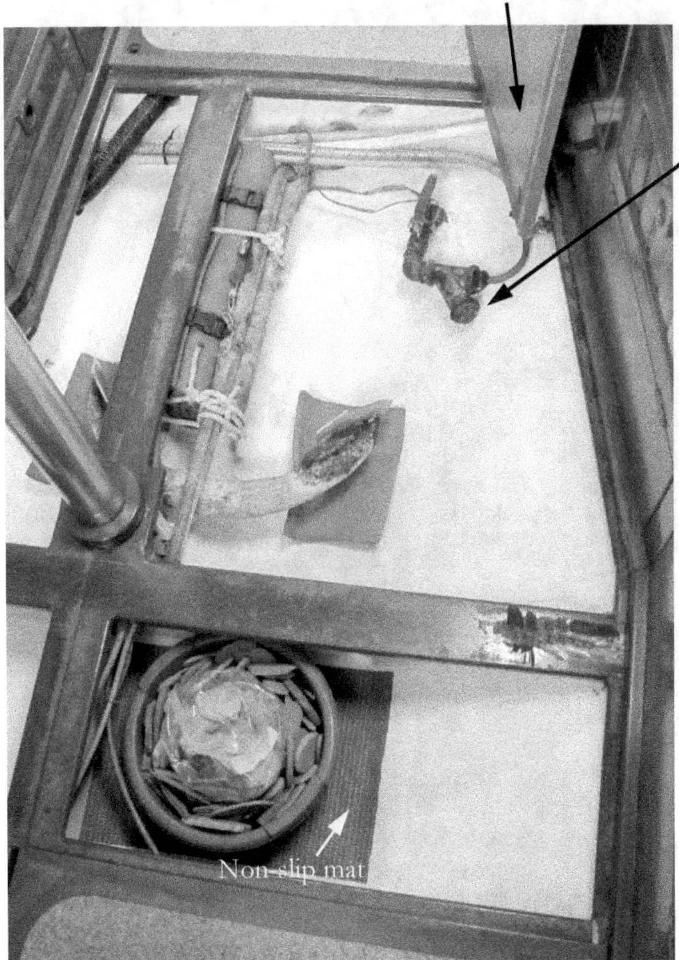

Seawater valve supplies both the head and galley.

Holding up the floor with one hand I can reach in and quickly shut the seawater intake valve; so it's no hassle to close at any time.

Spare anchor stows easily and can be accessed quickly.

Under all floors can be quickly checked in an emergency. Nothing is stowed on the floor that could prevent lifting it.

The Spare Anchor

Rolled up camp mat with small pieces under the flukes keeps this anchor snug. One anchor fluke passes through a hole in the floor thwart. Silver rope with the soft mat pulls the anchor up tight against the centre thwart.

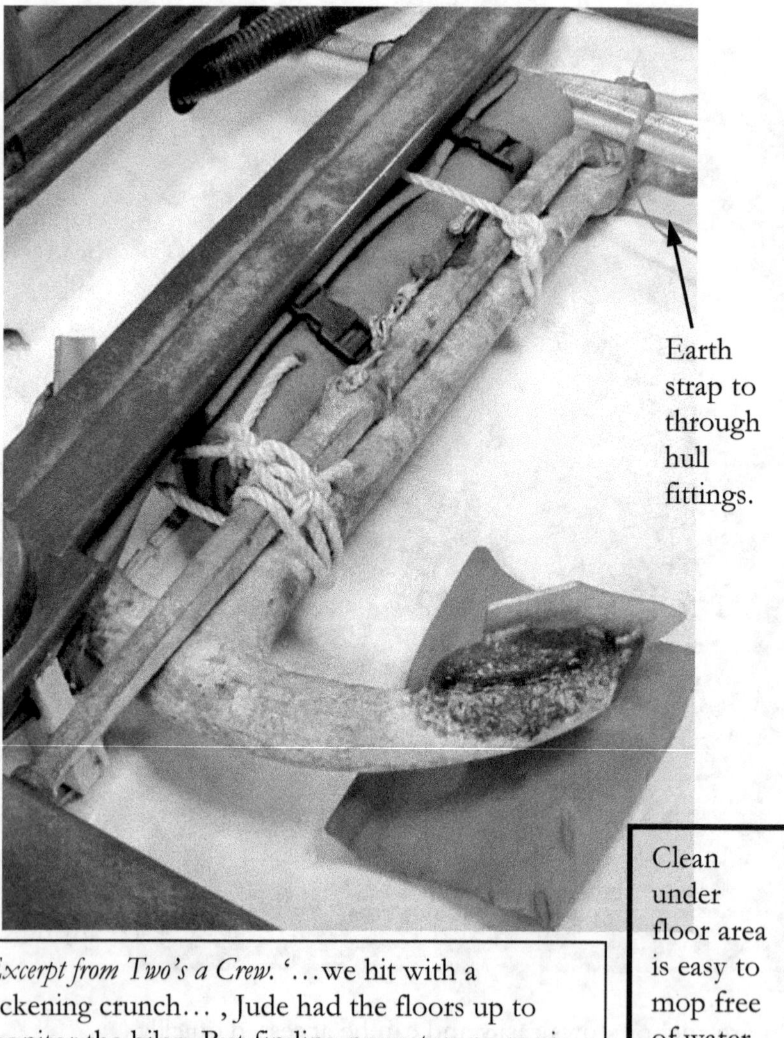

Earth strap to through hull fittings.

Clean under floor area is easy to mop free of water ingress.

Excerpt from Two's a Crew. '…we hit with a sickening crunch… , Jude had the floors up to monitor the bilge. But finding no water, no panic, just urgency. If we didn't get off, we'd fall over…, break off the mast.'

The Depth Sounder

Saloon drawers slide out and ply top hinges up to reveal the depth sounder.

The top drawer contains easy to get to goodies for the watch keeper at night. The bottom drawer is handy for honey and jars of niceties used at mealtimes. Drawers have slide bolt locks.

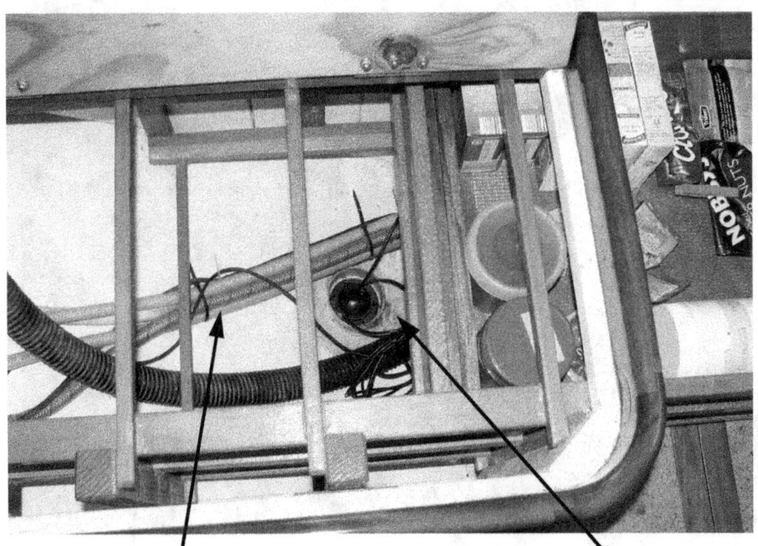

Hot and cold fresh water hoses. Depth sounder.

The Ship's Log

This is the bottom of the saloon locker. It lifts for hull access.

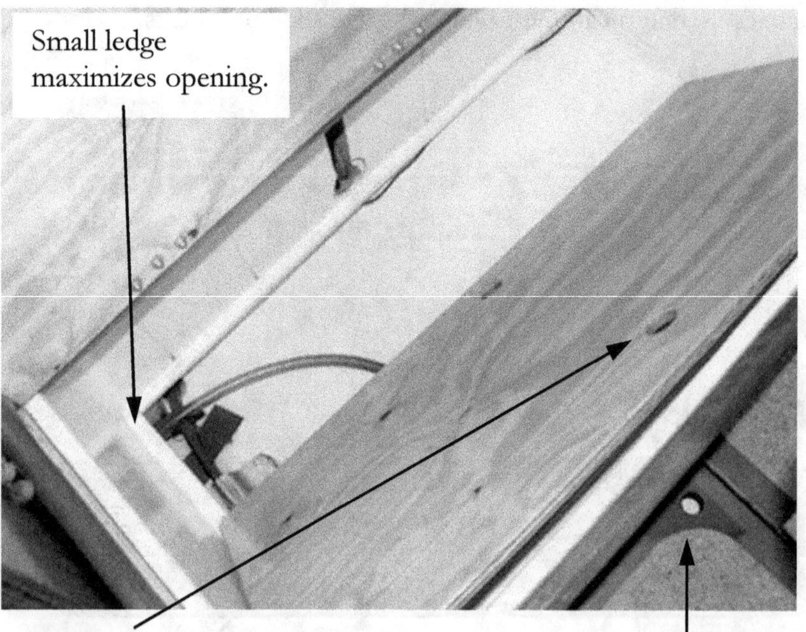

Finger holes in cupboard base and in saloon floor make lifting up easy. All floors have finger holes.

The Foot Pumps

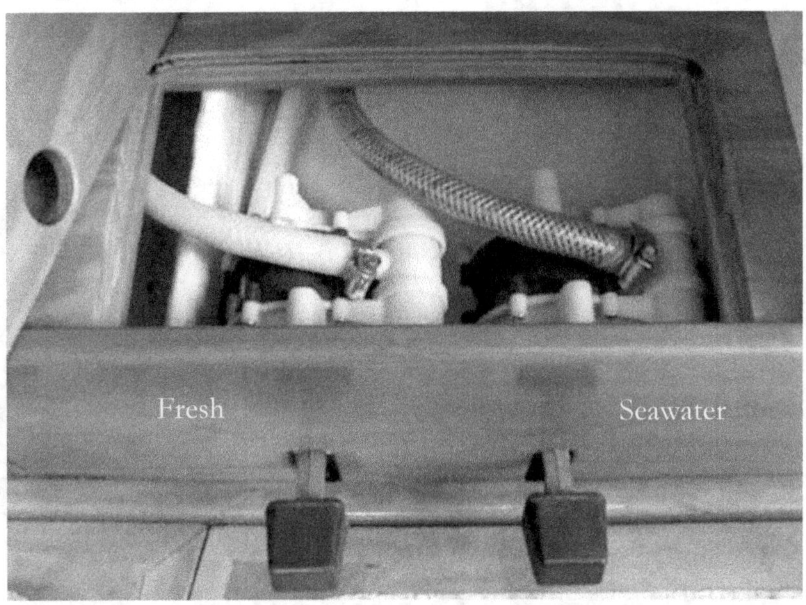

Cut out in the bottom galley shelf accesses the foot pumps. Left pump is fresh water. Right pump is seawater.

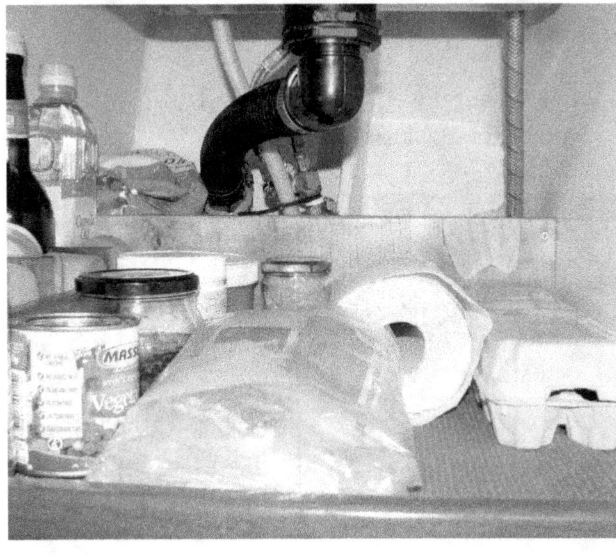

A deep fiddle towards the back of the top shelf allows easy access to the sink outlet valve and view of hull.

I stow low height items such as eggs and bread here.

The Hull Behind Shelves

Shelves in the forward cabin cupboards are removable for full access to hull.

When I periodically empty and sort; it's a simple task to examine the hull.

Two no 8 screws hold it in place along the cupboard front.

And one screw at each end fixes it down to small ledges on the cupboard sides.

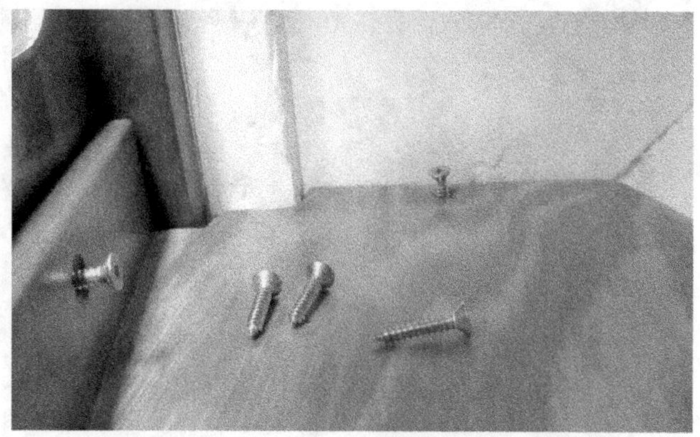

Non-slip mat does what it's supposed to do, but it also stops small bits getting lodged at the back of the shelf.

Tip. Inaccessible voids left empty helps stop the boat getting stuffy; like those below the forward cabin shelves and under the galley shelves.

Drop Down Cupboard Doors

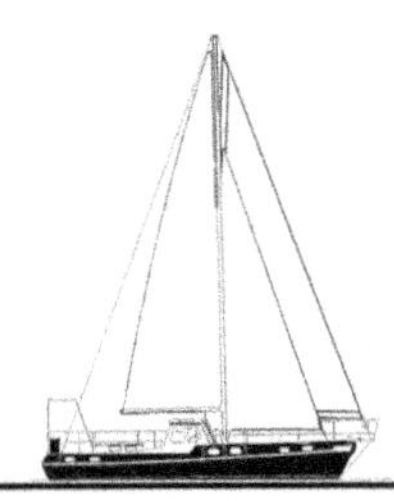

Drop down cupboard doors work well in narrow spaces especially between forward V bunks.

The bottom doors clear the floor and do not intrude into the floor area when open.

Bunk mattresses are on slat bases with hinged sections allowing access to the top shelf/as well as through the door.

Really useful if a guest comes aboard with a suitcase!!! The suitcase drops in and there's little need to unpack.

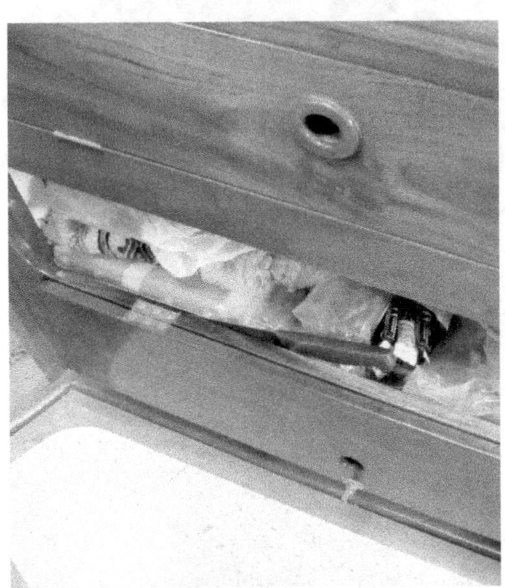

Tip. Design mattresses so they can be turned over to prevent mould.

Tip. Store light things forward and heavier things amidships.

Slat Bunk Tops & Ventilation

Slat Bunk Tops and voids under bottom shelves helps ventilation.

The Head

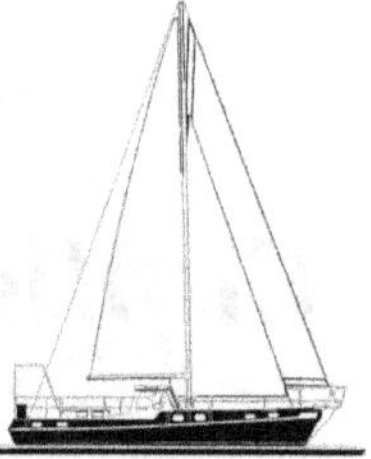

Please remember, -- don't forget! Never leave the bathroom wet,

Nor leave the soap still in the water –

That's the thing you never ought'er! –

And as you've been so often told,

Never let the hot run cold;

Nor leave the towels upon the floor,

Nor keep the bath an hour or more……..

Bathrooms on boats should be light, airy, easy to keep clean and well ventilated. There are no dark, damp places for cockies here.

Home Made LAVAC

The head is a homebuilt Lavac operated by a Henderson pump Mk III or IV.

The large capacity has meant no blockages.

The little cupboard behind the toilet is self-draining and doubles as a backrest.

Note the rubber pad on a block of wood below it. The toilet seat rests on it when up.

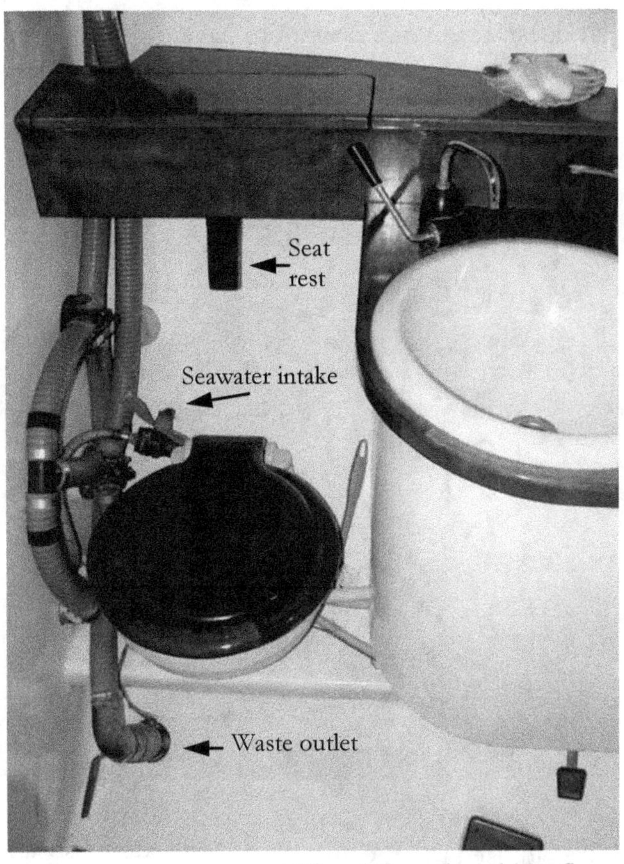

The toilet plumbing is three way. Overboard – To sullage – Or pumpout.

The sink pedestal is a flat fibreglass sheet pulled round and glued to rims top and bottom.

The plumbing inside is accessed from underneath.

There's no cupboard here, so nothing to wet.

A gap behind the toilet base lets shower water drain down the hull.

All through-hull sea cocks are visible. Valves open or closed seen at a glance.

A red ribbon reminds us to shut off the seawater intake.

The Shower

It doesn't take much room to have a shower. Note the foot rule on the floor grate. Swinging room for the arms is all we need.... The toilet seat is good to put the foot on.

All bathroom corners are radiused to prevent moisture retention.

Door jamb slopes in and down so water drains inside.

A simple sponge down after a shower keeps this head clean.

Last one in cleans up.

Below the sink.

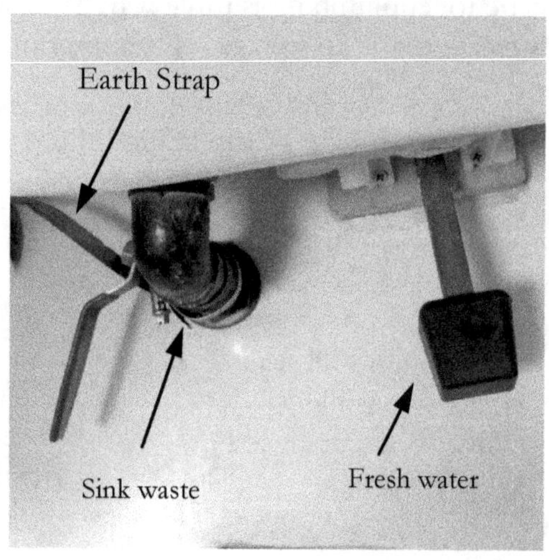

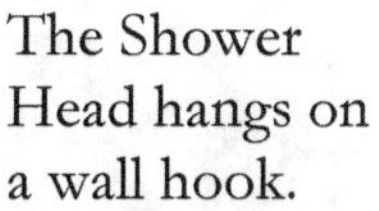

The Shower Head hangs on a wall hook.

The fittings screw onto the faucet when needed.

It is always stowed at sea in the top cupboard.

After many years without hot water we now have a 30 L system which works off the engine or shore power.

It takes just 20 minutes of engine running, like coming in to anchor, for us both to have a hot shower.

When sailing in the tropics, it didn't matter not having a shower. Now, sailing cold climates – with aging bodies, what a boon!

Ventilation

Deck hatch airs the head out quickly.

The door to the head can be hooked ajar and the hatch left open to aid ventilation through the boat in hot climates.

Mosquito Nets

The rebate in the hatch trim holds up the mosquito net.

All hatches in *Banyandah* have rebated trims.

See next page for details.

Mosquito Nets

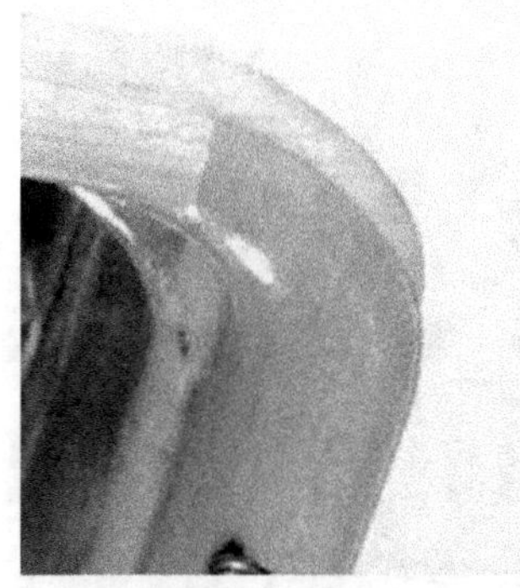

Rebated hatch trim for mosquito net.

The timber surround also holds the head liner in place.

How To Make Mosquito Nets

Cut a rectangle or square 20 mm bigger than the inside of the hatch surround out of midge netting (used on camper vans). Black is perfect - it doesn't stand out like a sore thumb in the night light.

Round the corners to suit.

Stitch a belt of material around the edge of the netting – taking in a 10 mm seam. I have used calico which blends well with the head liner.

I've done some nip and tucking and a bit of gathering around the corners to get it to fit, so that when the net is up it's stretched taut.

Now turn a hem around the outer edge and slot 3 - 4 mm light duty shock cord through. Remember when you cut the calico to size that it has to go round the edge of the trim and back into the groove.

Tip. Once the cord is tensioned correctly, sew a line of stitching inside it to keep the cord toward the outer edge.

Cupboards

Small bathroom cupboard for toothpaste, toothbrushes, hairbrush, etc.

Gutters each end keeps shower water out.

Note the drain holes in the bottom - put there just in case.

This is one of only four high cupboards in *Banyandah.*

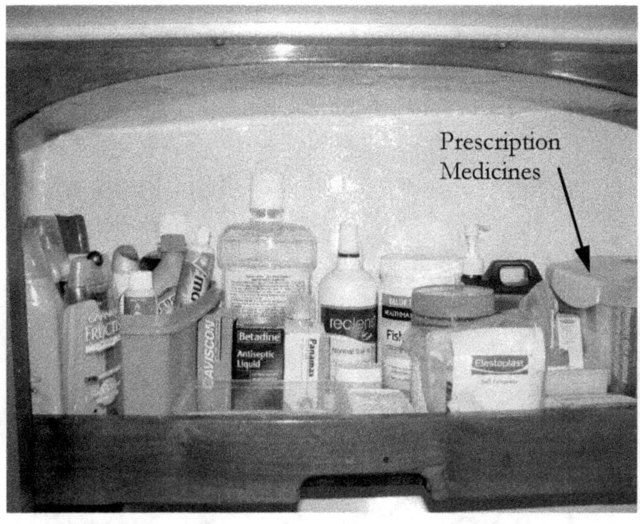

Prescription Medicines

Not for everyday use, stored in their own container.

Tip.

Keep an original copy of prescription medicines inside the box.

This is where we'll find everyday essentials - antiseptic, band-aids, lotions and ointments – plus a large bottle of normal saline for urgent use. Towels are kept elsewhere.

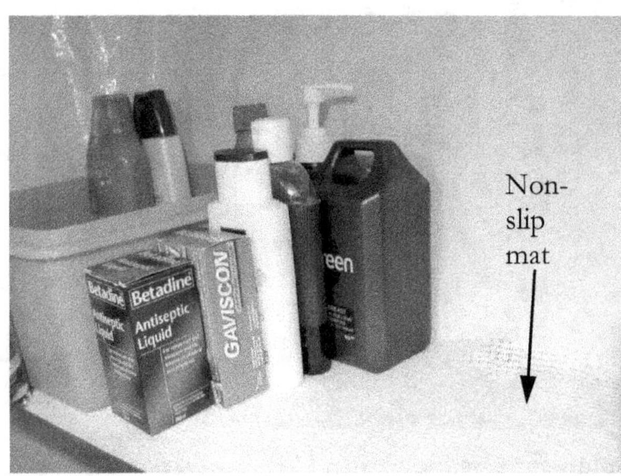

A hand can 'plunge' the sunscreen without it being removed.

Dry Food Lockers

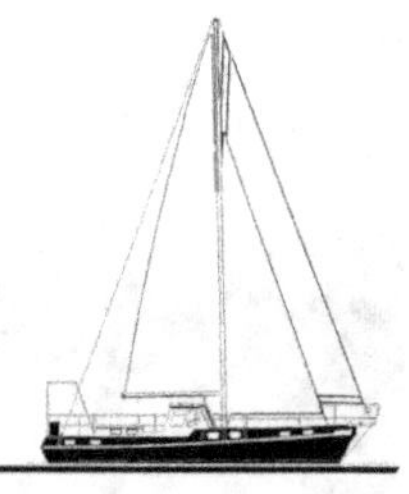

This dry food storage locker under a seat is fully sealed against possible ingress of water from below floor level.

The hull is protected with outdoor carpet.

Next to the galley, it's easily accessible for everyday dry goods.

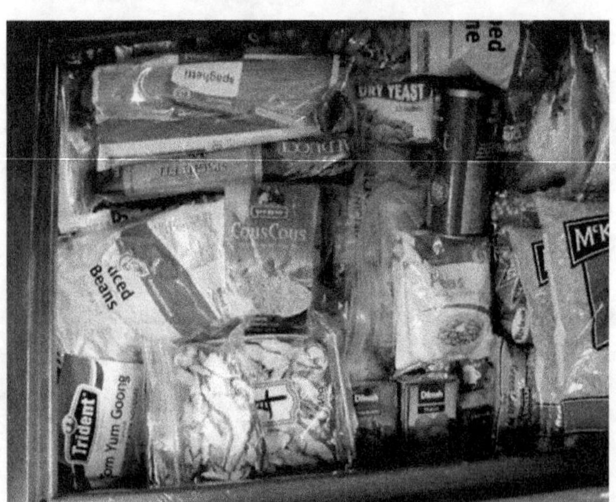

Cruising long term, it's impossible to store everything in separate screw top containers.

> ***Tip.***
>
> **Zip-lock** bags are useful for storing dry goods weighing less than 1 kg.

Let's Have Breakfast

Large volumes, such as flour, cracker biscuits, cereals and grains are stored in their own containers below this saloon seat which is opened less frequently.

This 'Breakfast Locker' works really well. Open cereal boxes don't have to be lifted out for use – so there's no danger of spillage at sea. Jack and I take our bowls to the boxes.

Bottles in sock muffs.

Tall bottles are stored amongst the plastic cereal containers. Homemade bottled tuna stows in the corner. Old socks protects the glass.

This large rectangular locker is almost amidships. It's a great place to store my seldom used Eski – in which I store packets of cracker biscuits.

Sock-It

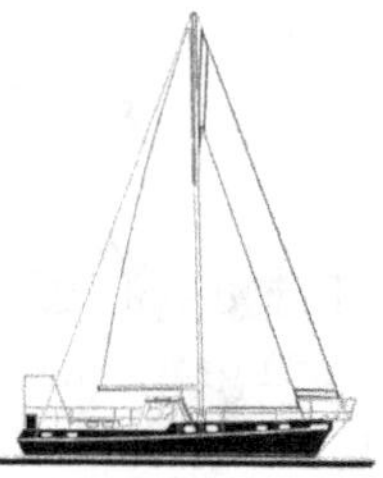

Old socks make good muffs.

Protect glass bottles.

Cut the socks into two or three pieces. Stretch onto the bottle or drop bottle into the foot part.

Alternate muffed bottles within the cupboard to save socks.

This plastic storage box lives in the forward end of the cockpit locker galley side. It nests against my hard vegetables bin. When Banyandah was re-fitted her cockpit lockers were built to suit bin size commonly available.

Handles for easy lifting out.

Sock the Glass Coffee Jug

Tip. Put a sock on any item that might roll around to keep it quiet.

The glass coffee maker stores upright in the galley cupboard. It has its own wide rubber base and sits on non-slip mat when stowed.

The muff is left on when in use, which helps keep the coffee hot.

The odd can clunking in a cupboard can be muffed too but if the socks become wet the cans rust quickly.

Non-Slip Mat

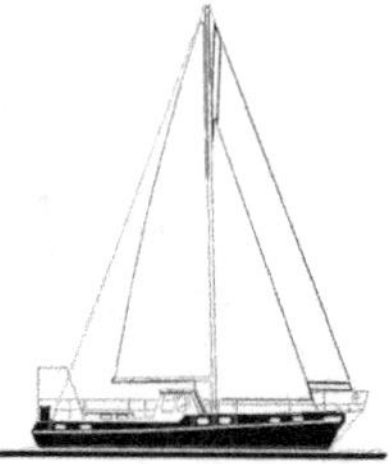

Line the galley bench.

Imagine how much stuff could fall off the galley benches when passage making. The stainless steel bench is easy to keep clean.

The top bench has non-slip mat and fiddles, and works well. All tops hinge open and are fully guttered so spills run back onto the bench and not into the cupboards.

The top opening fridge lies on the other side of the stove aft.

Tip. A piece of non-slip mat in the bottom of the sink works well too.

Non-slip Mat in the Galley

Non-slip mat on the galley bench works very well.

The flat tray stays put when the boat is under way.

Non-slip comes in 300 mm wide rolls and can be bought from warehouse type stores. Wider material is available at ship chandlers.

Line shelves and drawers with non-slip mat.

Tip. A piece of non-slip mat can be used to wash dishes.

Non-slip along the Top Hinging Top Benches.

The top cupboards go only as deep as the galley benchtop so they are easy to reach into.

Top hinging gives access to otherwise lost space beside the plates.

This little space is perfect for bowls.

Anything spilt runs down the gutter onto the galley bench.

A rolled up tea towel stops dishes from sliding/and different sizes can be accommodated.

Tip. Below the large plates is a set of slightly smaller ones that are useful when I need a lot of plates on the saloon table. A piece of non-slip mat between the two sets keeps the lot still.

In the Cockpit

500 mm wide non-slip has been used here. Sunglasses can be safely put down.

On the Cabin Sole

> ***Tip.*** A piece of non-slip cut slightly smaller than a soft floor mat is surprisingly good at keeping it in one spot.
> Cosy comfort for the feet on a cold night at anchor.

The Galley

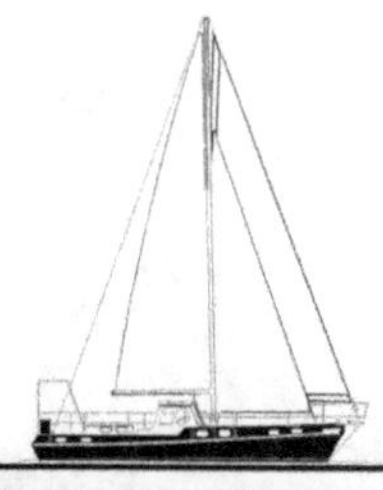

The Safety Strap

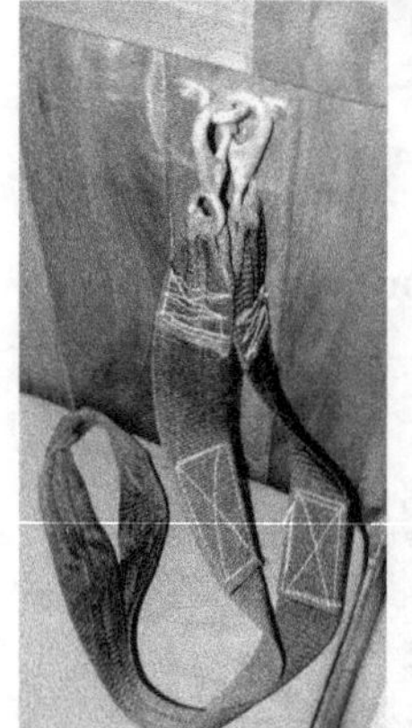

The safety strap clips around the front of the galley to the right of the drawers.

In really heavy weather on the starboard tack I'm safe in the galley.

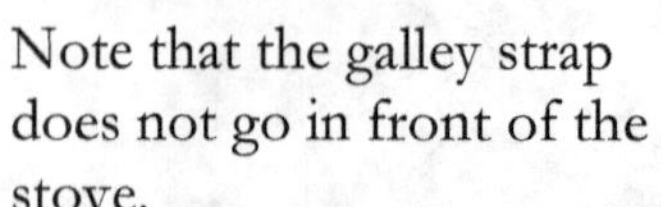

Note that the galley strap does not go in front of the stove.

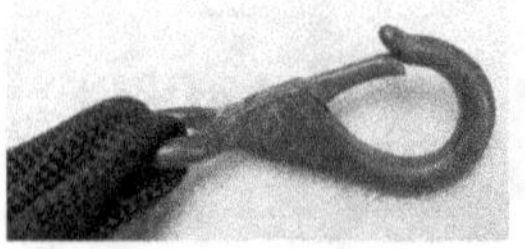

The Sink and Seawater Tap

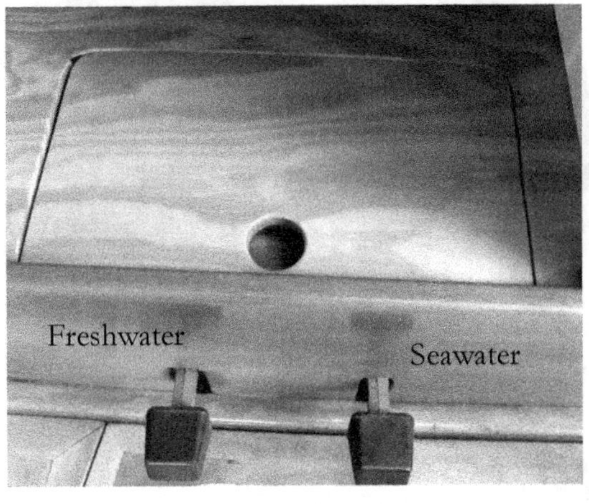

Seawater in the galley saves fresh water. When not in confined or possibly contaminated waters I use it to wash dishes.

The single sink is a good size. 380x340x150 mm. The drain is in the centre.
A small bowl 310 mm for washing up saves fresh water. Dishes drain around the sides. The right nozzle is for seawater, foot operated, so no handle intrudes into the galley bench. The left handpump runs from a foot pump, it's fresh water. The centre mixer is for pressure hot and cold for those odd times of luxury when we have running hot water. The mixer faucet is one used in any standard kitchen with low cutoff pressure.

Bottom shelves throughout the boat are all well above floor level. A void space below helps with ventilation. This cut out accesses the foot pumps for maintenance.

Gutters & Bungs

Banyandah has 4 individual water tanks, two each side. Sometimes when heeled over, if the tank on the upside is on, it will drain out the downside faucet.

Drain hole in the galley bench for just such a mishap.

Bung it

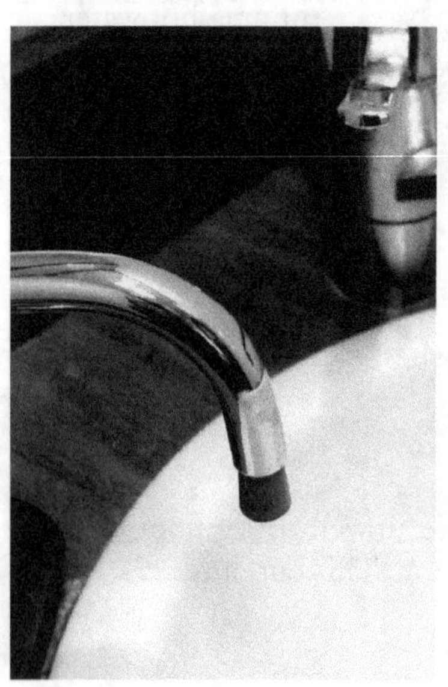

We bung all water outlets automatically before leaving an anchorage.

Cutlery

The top cutlery drawer, 6 sections of 5 mm wood held in with liquid nails. T-towels are behind the back divider – not quite visible.

Keep the drawer lightweight for everyday use.

A small piece of outdoor carpet is in each section to help keep the cutlery still.

All drawers have slide bolts for security while underway.

Below the drawers is a cupboard with a drop down door.

This drawer is athwart the ship so arranging the cutlery fore and aft has worked out well.

The size of sections 1, 2, 3, 4 and 5 are dependant on length of cutlery.

Heavy lines are sides that are taller to contain the bigger utensils.

The dashed line is the drawer interior.

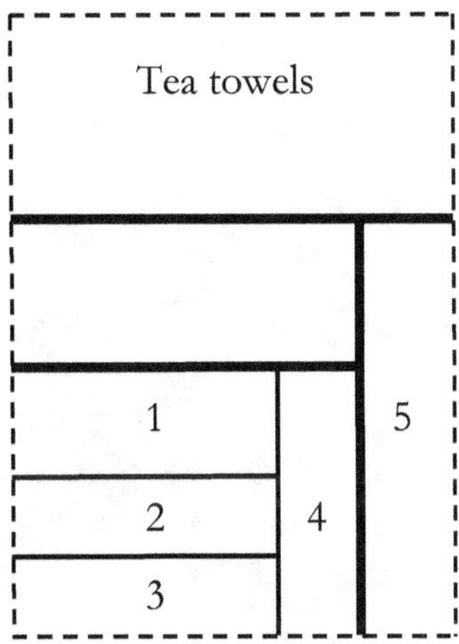

The Stove

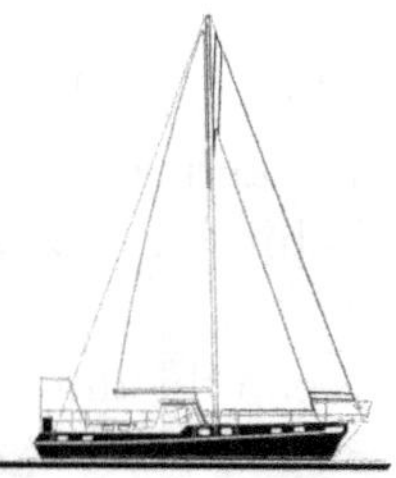

The gimballed stove has a slide bolt lock at the bottom. Alongside, or when at anchor, and visitors come I can lock it to be sure it cannot be tipped accidentally.

Deep fiddles and locking bars secure pans.

This pan has been aboard nearly forty years. It is my favourite and the most used.

For extra security the pan handles can clip to the fiddles. A hook each end of a shockcord does the trick.

Tip. A deep wide pan with open handles is a must on every serious cruiser.

Liquids don't slop out.

The gas turn off is behind the galley.

Don't Burn The Bread

A Problem

This Broadwater SS stove replaced my old rusted Roden Rambler and fit the same space but came with two problems.

1/ The oven burner protrudes up into the oven space as opposed to being below. And the bread burnt even though the temperature was turned down low.

2/ Only one shelf can be used!

The Solution

Place a piece of alloy 20 mm thick and about 20 mm wider and 10 mm deeper on top of the burner plate to dissipate the heat.

The gap at the back has been retained.

However it has not solved the problem of the reduction in oven size.

The Fridge

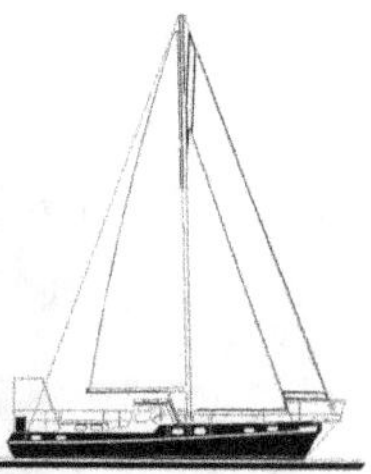

Note the fridge on/off switch on the galley bulkhead.

The fridge on *Banyandah* runs on a Danfoss System pumping refridgeration through a glycol solution creating a eutectic plate which is the cold sink.

It works on 12v. It is switched on for an hour or two each day depending on ambient temperature. This is usually when we start the engine to leave an anchorage, or when the sun is up enough to charge the batteries via our 240 w of solar cells.

We have two banks of batteries, 3 general usage, and 2 under the forward steps that power the anchor winch and can also be used for engine starting.

The isolating switch for the anchor winch batteries is convenient and easy to see its on/off status.

The Fridge

If you like freedom away from your boat *like we do* then the fridge should not be too big. It should also be well insulated and preferably top opening as cold sinks.

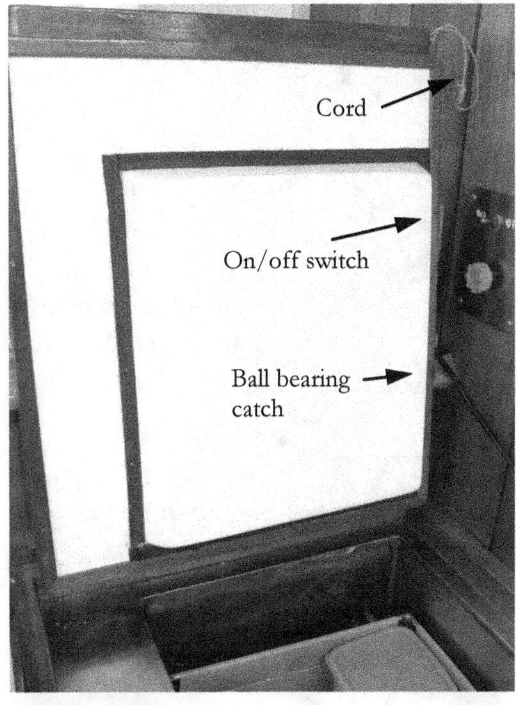

Ideal depth inside is 650 mm from top open surface. My fingers can reach the bottom.

There is at least 100 mm of insulation all round with more than 150 mm at the back and bottom filling the voids to the hull.

Insulation on the right side of the box extends through the thickness of the bulkhead, hence its lopsided look when open.

Spring loaded pin hinge. The door can come off.

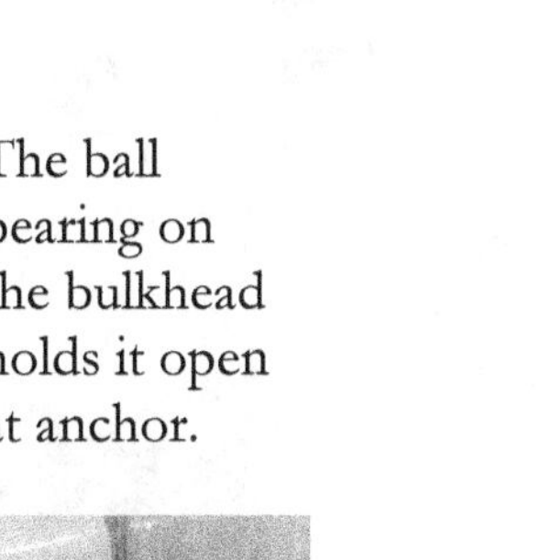

The ball bearing on the bulkhead holds it open at anchor.

3 mm cord permanently attached to the door hooks over an 8 mm round head screw on the bulkhead to keep it open when at sea.

The gas piping is out of harms way.

At a glance I can see if it's frosting when on.

The cooling pipes go out the side of the box and through the insulated bulkhead directly into the Danfoss unit mounted on the other side in the cockpit locker.

That cockpit locker is designated galley storage and where hard vegetables are stored.

The eutectic plate compartment is full.

The cans sit on non-slip mat.

Another piece of mat on top stops those lying down from shifting.

Perfect. The beer, nice and cold also acts as a cold sink.

The eutectic plate will freeze food stored in it, but we have no need to keep food frozen as we don't eat meat.

If we catch a fish too large for more than a few meals – out comes the pressure cooker to preserve the rest in bottling jars. Meat and chicken can also be preserved in bottling jars.

We like to share a fish with the mutton birds.

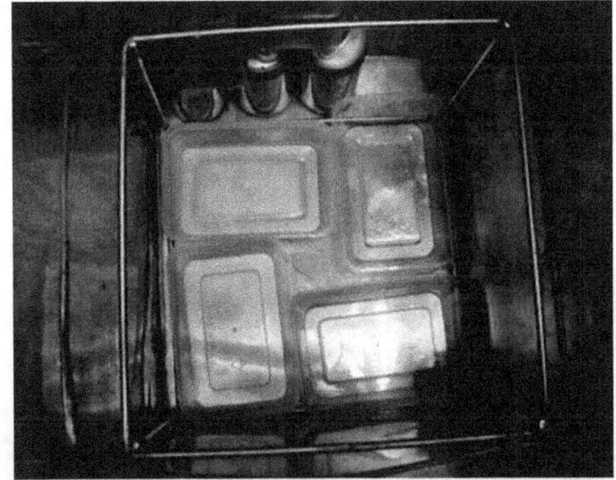

Plastic containers keep stowed cheese off the bottom and lets condensation drain.

Vegetables such as cauliflower and tomatoes rest on top.

The bottom basket is not lined – so there's no vinyl to sit in any moisture.

This frame is there just to hold up the top two baskets.

Square water bottles fill the void behind and keep baskets in place when underway.

A top opening fridge separate from the galley bench is best. Nothing need be moved to get into it. No spilt liquids seep into it.

Tip. Keeping the fridge fairly full with bottles of liquid is a good way to prevent loss of coldness when the fridge is opened.

Total standing height of the three baskets equals 595 mm.

Depth inside fridge is 650 mm from top surface when lid is open.

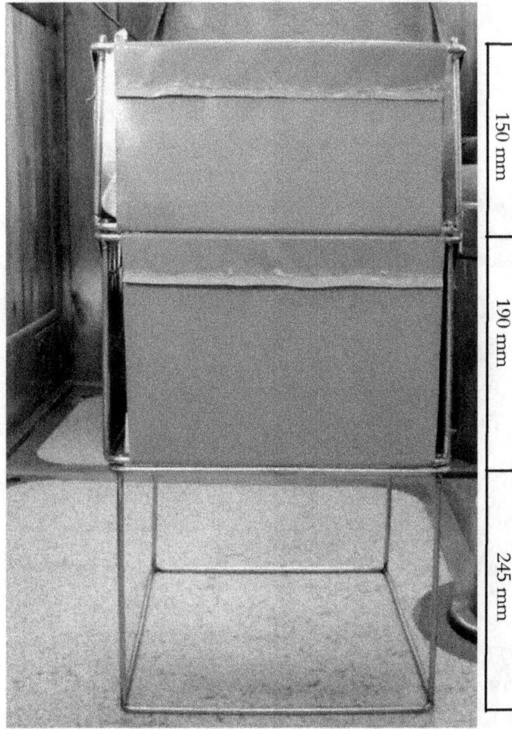

Basket size: outside, 305 mm square x 5 mm SS rod.

Fridge inside: 315 mm wide by about 410 mm front to back. This allows the lid plug to drop in and space for the baskets to lift in and out.

A length of vinyl is stretched around the basket then hand stitched on.

A second layer is sewn on the opposite way. These two layers give the bottom rigidity.

The bottom frame is deep. Bulky vegetables will store here.

The other two baskets of different heights interchange depending on how I want to use them.

The top basket gets used for everyday items and is not heavy to lift out.

Basket Detail

The 5-6 mm rod stands up about 10 mm at each corner of every basket. They interlock the baskets together and hold them in position.

The Baskets in my fridge are brilliant.

The baskets, well vented at each corner, lets cold air circulate freely between the inside of the baskets and the fridge box.

Food inside stays more uniformly cold.

Food does not rest against the inside of the fridge box.

Food is more easily kept separate from another.

Jack and I both know which level certain foods are stored on – so little time is taken to get out what we want – and less cold is lost.

Power consumption is kept to a minimum.

Tip. Place a piece of paper towel in the bottom of each basket to soak up any moisture.

The Eutectic Plate shaped in a 'U' forms the freezer box (used as a cold box on our boat – although we've been known to freeze a beer when left on too long).
It's located at the top back of the fridge because cold sinks.

The inside of the box size is
245 mm high x 240 mm wide and 235 mm front to back and has a fiddle at the front.

Tip. Before leaving the boat for a few days I fill all vacant space with bottles of water (and beer) and make sure the eutectic plate freezes. Then I put a thick towel in the top. That way I don't lose all my valuable vegetables especially when in isolated places.
This worked well in the Kimberley where it was very hot. When we returned after a three day bushwalk looking for Bradshaw Art, we enjoyed a cold beer. The vegetables had not suffered – which was good for us because the next place with fresh produce was not until Dampier many weeks later.

Fridge Drainage

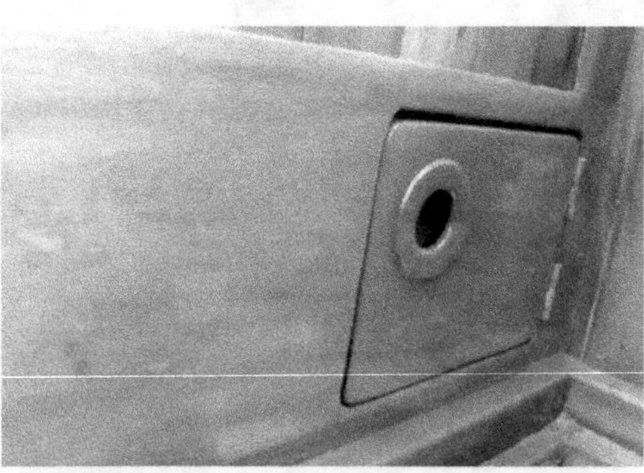

Easy:

Open the little door at the bottom of the fridge.

Hold an old juice bottle cut off at the neck to catch any condensation.

Open the ball valve.

The fridge never smells.

The fridge bottom is so well insulated I don't feel the drain compromises the fridge coldness.

Baskets

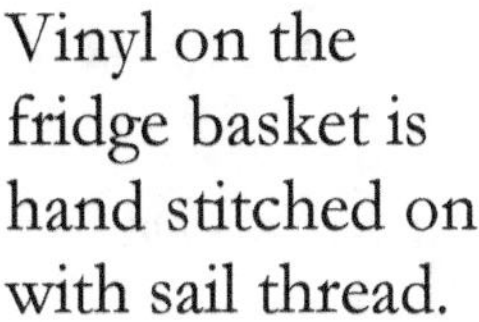

Vinyl on the fridge basket is hand stitched on with sail thread.

This wicker tray sits on the top bench close to the fridge and never slides. It is handy for those bits of fruit that need to be eaten first. I'm never tempted to overfill it.

Hanging nets for fruit and vegetable tend to swing around too much and if the fruit is soft it bruises and spoils.

Garbage and Cockies

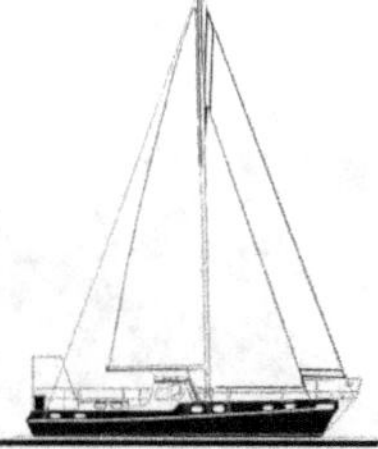

Garbage

Leave it Ashore

Minimise the garbage that you bring on board in the first place.

Select products with minimal packaging, if you can, when shopping. You not only have to carry it back to the boat as extra weight, but then you have to dispose of it too somewhere down the track. – When packing your goods into bags, take a moment to dispose of all the extra packing; leave it behind in the supermarket bins.

I have a large number of green 'eco' bags in use. I rarely bring plastic shopping bags back to the boat.

Storing Garbage on board

Storing garbage on the boat takes space.

Salt water available in the galley is wonderful for saving fresh water. Wash out tins, bottles and even plastic bags before storing.
Bad smells on boats are not nice.

Compress cans especially aluminium.

Sort waste as it accumulates. Keep food scraps separate. Scraps that go ashore do so in an old jar and that includes waste cooking oils.

A narrow plastic bag such as the type a loaf of bread comes in from the market is a perfect one for compressing clean rubbish into.

> ***Tip.*** Don't throw vegetable waste overboard while at anchor or close to shore, it floats ashore and if it sinks it looks horrible.

Cockroaches

Cockroaches are hard to exterminate

When we left *Banyandah* on the hard in Albany for the winter, we had just sailed out of the tropics, and unfortunately we had a few cockroaches on board.

I did a thorough spring clean before we left and packed leftover dry goods that were still well in date into tins.

The eski, stowed in our breakfast locker under the saloon seat was packed full then I ran a double sealing tape around its lid.

Then when we left I placed about thirty-six cockroach hotels around the boat.

We returned to no signs of the pests, except a few dead ones. *That is now three years ago.*

I was so pleased with the result that I went to the trouble of taking the headliner down from above the galley – or Jack did; he was installing some electrical wires. And I was even more delighted to find only one empty cockroach sack; presumably hatched and then killed by the baits.

Tip. Don't bring cardboard boxes on board. They can be infested with cockroaches.

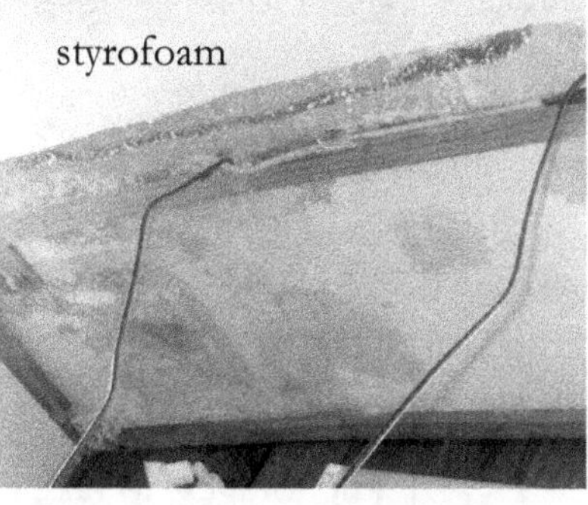

Broccoli box used as insulation above head liner works well.

Tip. If you leave your boat for an extended period of time store all your dry food in tins or plastic containers; including food in zip-lock bags. Cockroaches can eat through packaging.

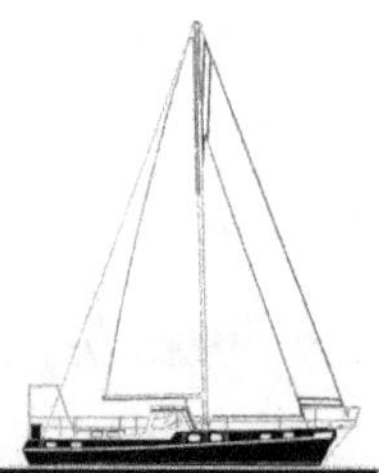

First Aid/ Torches

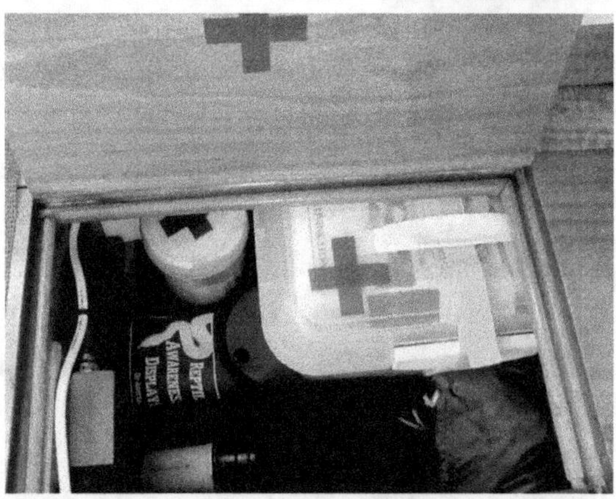

This top opening locker behind the fridge contains:

Torches

A pocket knife

A comprehensive First Aid Kit in a see through plastic box – to grab quickly if needed for use on boat or ashore.

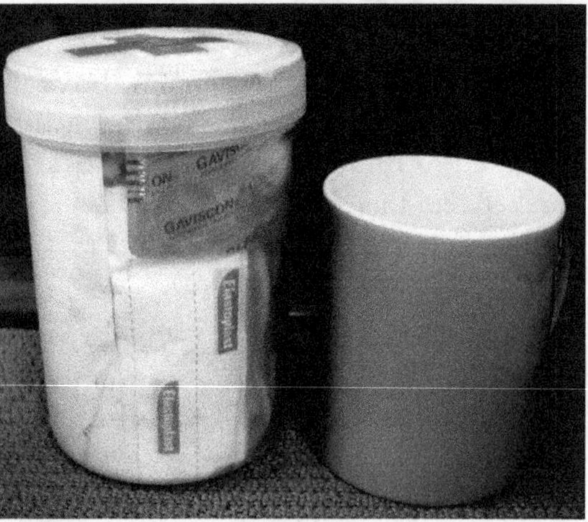

Most often when we go ashore we take the small first aid kit and a container of water.

The small First Aid Kit in a drum 100 mm x 140 mm. It's amazing how much is in this drum. It even includes an eye bathing kit, steri-strip sutures, pain killers and antihistamine.

When going ashore at an isolated anchorage we also take the knife, a PLB and torch.
You just never know!

Tip. Make it a habit when you go ashore, particularly in isolated anchorages, to take emergency equipment with you. You'll be glad of the torch if you're late back, if only to find the dinghy.

Curtains

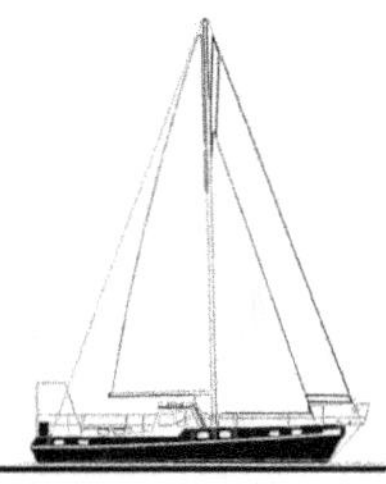

Stretch curtains across ports easily when privacy is required, or leave up permanently.

Calico allows some light in.

Fix a stainless steel round headed screw each side of the window. Leave a 3 mm gap behind.

Remove curtains without leaving unsightly wire or pelmets.

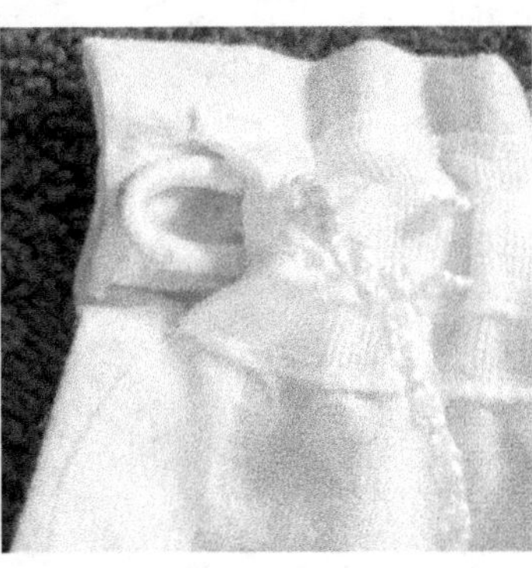

Slot 3 mm white shock cord (the type bought from sewing supply stores) through the curtain tape. Make a loop each end.

Sew in place after first stretching across the window to fit.

Slip loops over screws.

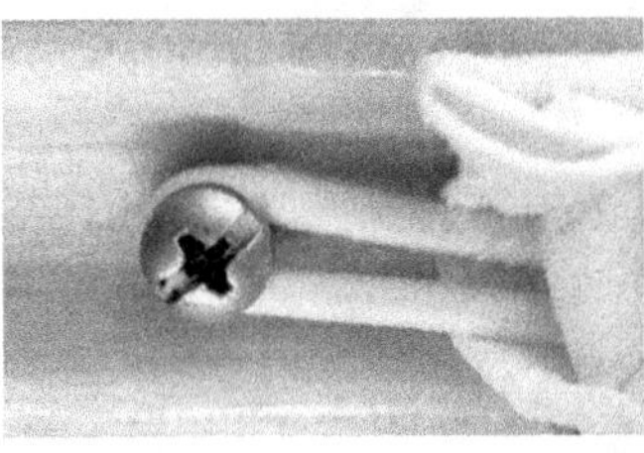

Tip. Initially calico needs to be washed and ironed. But after that I just give them a good shake after washing.

Centre Cockpit

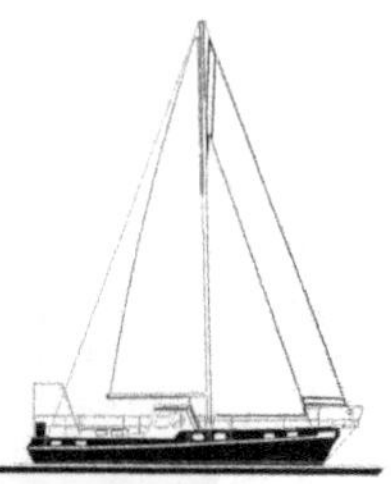

Lying alongside on a low tide at Stanley, Tasmania in sailing mode. Next destination: Three Hummocks. The dinghy is stowed on deck.

Spacious Cockpit and Hard Dodger with sliding hatch.

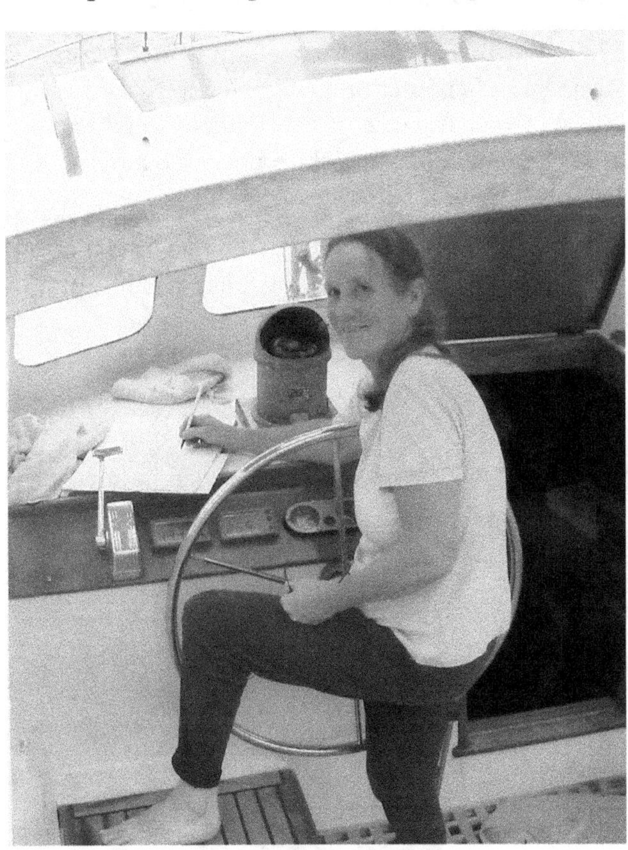

The ship's wheel on its own bulkhead is perfect.

A free standing wheel on a pedestal would have cluttered our cockpit.

Even in wet weather I can mark the ship's log, taking final details of the voyage.

I'm well protected by the dodger.

Standing on the cockpit seat I have a secure position to steer from, and to observe hand signals when anchoring. The Perspex has been formed and shaped to suit the curvature of the dodger top by first making a former then we found a plastic's shop that used a pizza oven to warm the Perspex letting it take the shape.

No! The sliding hatch is not a guillotine!
A slide bolt locks it open or shut.

Open in hot weather provides good ventilation.

When the hatch is closed the helmsperson can still see the top of the mast and the mainsail.

Four drain holes keep the helm dry.

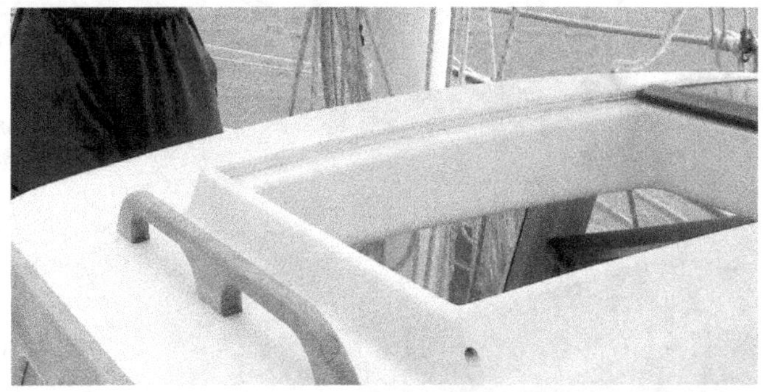

A fire extinguisher in the cockpit is essential in case of fire below.

The binocular case is permanently attached. We always know where they are and there's no danger of them falling.

Non-slip mat around the compass means sunglasses and other stuff can be safely put down. 500 mm wide non-slip has been used here.

The starboard cockpit locker is sectioned off using plastic storage containers with lids.

Longer keeping vegetables are stored in this locker in close proximity to the galley.

The aft seat locker contains tools, an assortment of spares and fishing gear.

Bin usually has non-slip mat in the bottom.

Jack checking the Danfoss refrigeration unit in the forward section.

Safety catch engages automatically when the locker is opened.

Made from a fiberglass offcut with a slot, it drops in place when the hatch is lifted.

Lift up when closing.

The port side cockpit lockers contain boat working gear; mooring lines, fenders, blocks of beer. Emergency Grab Bag sits on top at sea.

The Engine Room

The cockpit floor unbolts and lifts up for engine maintenance; but everyday access is through small double doors from stern cabin.

When the floor is up the edge rests in the cockpit drain gutter. A safety line is threaded through a bolt hole and tied to the hand railing. I don't have to worry about Jack losing his fingers.

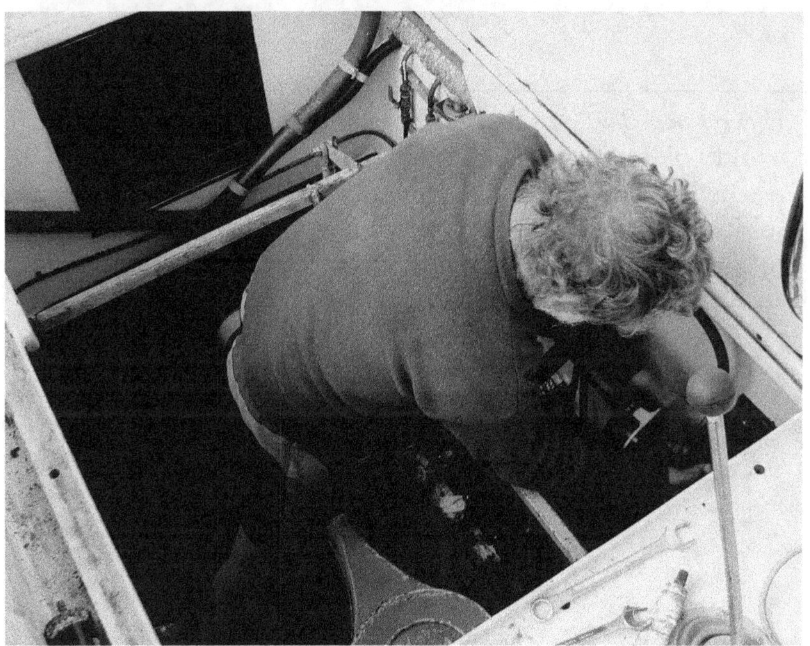

The floor, gutters, and frame are fiberglass for low mantainance. The lift up section has sound deadening material captured inside.

The floor gasket was formed in the floor itself using a pourable self-leveling Sikaflex type of material. The ridge that it sits on can be cleaned if necessary. It always beds down well.

Bolts with a flatwasher and rubber sealing washer drop in from the top and are fastened into captured nuts underneath.

This floor does not leak.

The Floor

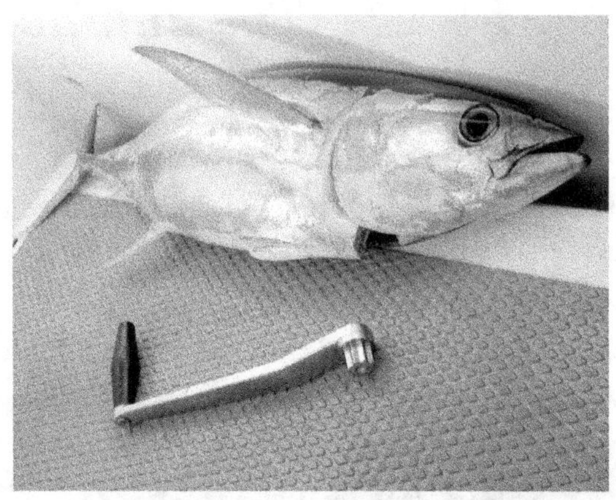

Excerpt from Two's a Crew. 'Hello from the tippy top of the world's oldest island. Once again *Banyandah* has successfully reached Torres Strait…… On board both oldies are in fine spirits and good health except for sore, tender feet caused by our new, overly aggressive, anti-skid cockpit flooring.

Jack spent a number of hours taking the sharp edges off each square of flooring.

He used a dowel wrapped with sandpaper.

Can't have the grandkids getting sore bums!

A Good Work Station

Maintaining a sheet winch in the cockpit.

Excerpt from Where Wild Winds Blow.

We'd not been on the water since tying our lady to the jetty half a year earlier. Sure, we'd done some maintenance and improvements; we'd put on new solar cells.

We went only as far as that cyclone hole near the river mouth, a weekend favourite for zooming speedboats towing screeching kiddies on inflatable rings. But before they arrived, Jude gasped between dives scraping barnacles from our through-hull fittings, while I tried to coax our windvane steering device to work freely again. The previous month's westerlies carrying heaps of central Australian dust into Mr. Aries innards had made him stiff. That dust had also seized up our poorly made Maxwell sheet winches, fizzing too many dissimilar metals of alloy, stainless and bronze into four mongrels of non-moving lumps.

Maintenance

Sail repairs out of the weather.

Maintaining the engine raw water pump.

Even the life ring should be checked frequently.

Companionway Doors

The aft sliding hatch is coated with Deks Olje.

No 1 matt only has been applied to the sliding hatch so it remains anti-slip.

No 2 gloss finish has also been applied on the doors.

Oil is not as hard wearing as varnish but is easier to maintain. Wash down with fresh water and when dry, wipe over with the oil. Follow directions on the can.

When these doors cannot be left open at sea we use this little hard rubber wedge to keep them closed.

The person below is not trapped. The door can be tapped open from inside.

A slide bolt locks the sliding hatch in place before the doors are closed and locked when leaving the boat.

The Aft Cabin

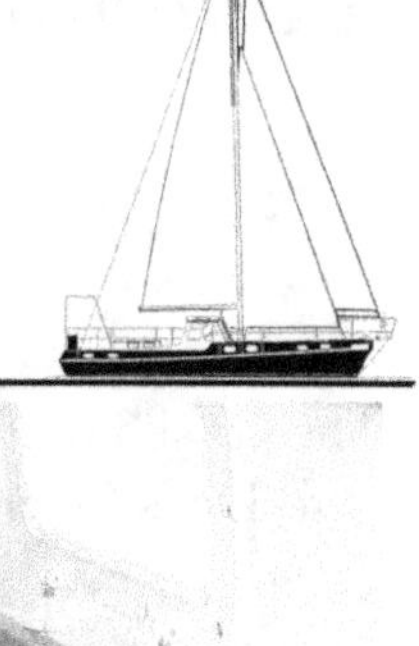

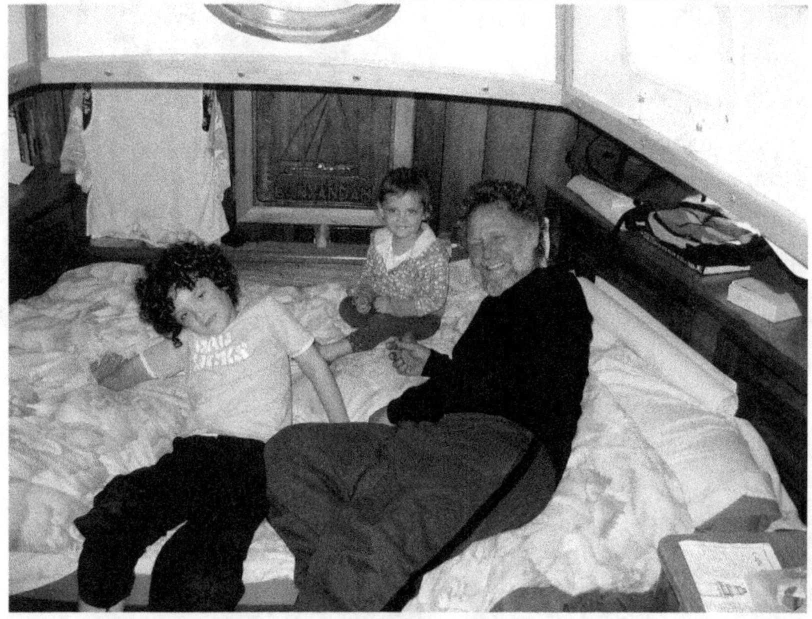

There are no fiddles on any bench top except the chart table. Only soft items or the odd book is placed on them. When the boat is being thrown about there's no risk of dangerous missiles.

We sleep athwartships at anchor, fore and aft at sea

We love having kids on board. There's plenty of room for them to lounge and they have their own quarters up forward in the V bunks.

Cupboards along the hull have drop down doors that lay flat on the bed so the hinges are not stressed.

The little top cupboard door also drops down.

and

The little cupboard door by the chart table hides the deck fill pipes for the water and fuel.

Always carry a good selection of paper charts.

Is the GPS system fool-proof in today's political climate or a lightning strike?

We used to have a hanging closet. It was a waste of space. We like the open feeling. We have only four cupboards high up in the boat. Two are in these pictures. I now hang the few blouses I need on the aft cabin bulkhead – previous page.

Tip. It's a good idea to have drawers that pull out from under the bed. We have two 350 mm wide. One stores linen, the other clothes and I don't have to pull the bed apart to get at them.

Looking forward into the cockpit.

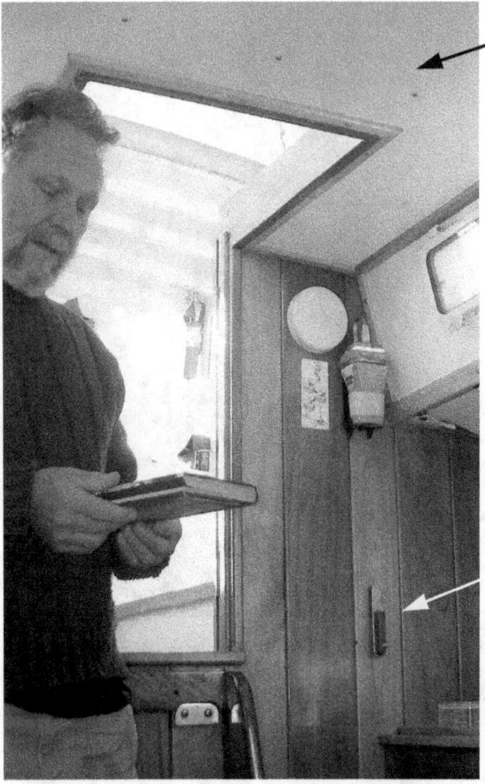

Home made headliner, 1 mm thick, was laid up on waxed whiteboard.

First tinted gel-coat then a layer of fiber-glass matt impregnated with resin. The slight dimple in the whiteboard takes the sheen off.

The EPIRB.

Central locking handle for the cockpit lockers – one each side.

A simple rod runs through the front edge of the lockers and when this handle is turned about 30 degrees, latches engage hooks.

The companionway ladder lifts off simple stainless steel homemade hooks for engine room access.

On the port bulkhead out of view is another fire extinguisher.

Safety Rails

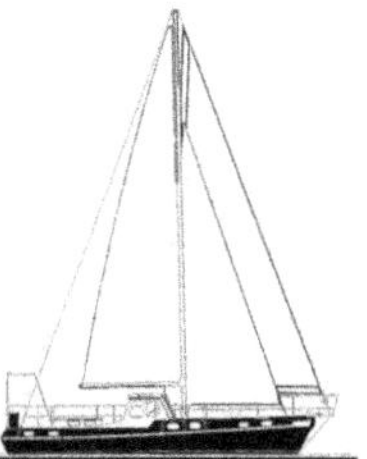

SS pipe boat railings are great. When working the deck at night and the boat lurches, the hand knows exactly where to catch hold.

And…. Well! With guests aboard they're more confident to move around the boat, and so are we to let them.

Hold On

The boarding ladder folds down and is permanently attached.

The safety chain holds it up.

When needed, a small cord cinches it tight and stops it rattling.

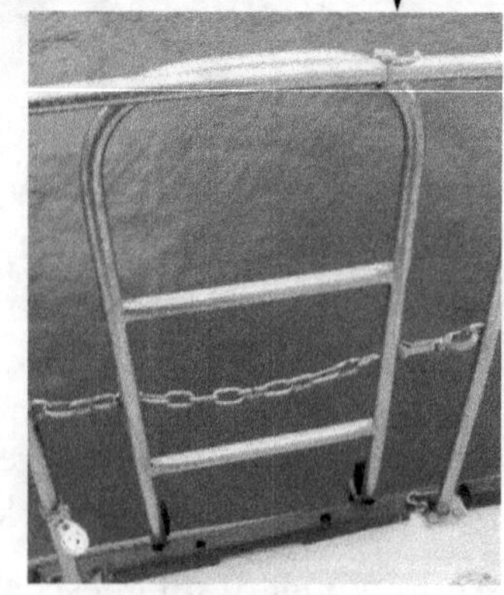

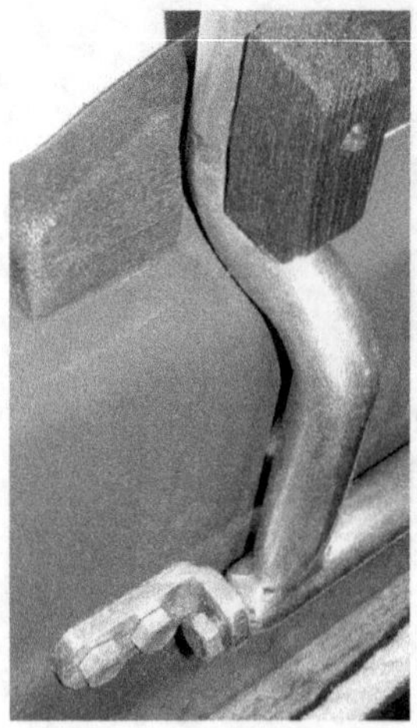

The hinge system is simple. An angled bracket bolts to the hull and the ladder.

Blocks rest against the rubbing strip in the down position.

The Aft Deck

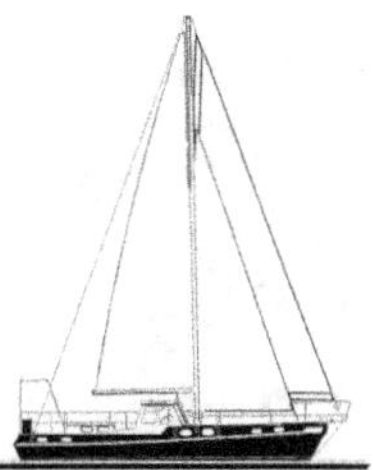

The Mosquito net over the stern sliding hatch is made from midge proof net, sewn into heavy duty calico.

3 mm stretch cord around the edge holds it on.

The hatch can still slide.

Tip. Slight notches cut in the threshold corners stops it slipping off.

Banyandah's stern deck is uncluttered.

The 6 man life raft is ready. Stern hatch slides under. A block system travels the main boom.

The Danforth anchor stows well on the poop rail. Flukes face outboard. Chain and rope stow in the deck locker.

Mobile phone antenna and solar cell anchor light are high up.

A Shady Seat under the tower.

The Aries easily handling fair Southern Ocean sailing.

Aries lines attach to the emergency tiller through blocks each side of the deck. Jam cleats used to adjust bias.

Shade is provided by canvas stretched taut under the solar cells.

Two permanent clothes lines athwart ship let the clothes fly with the wind. Clothes hanging along safety rails have a tendency to flip clothes pegs off and fly overboard.

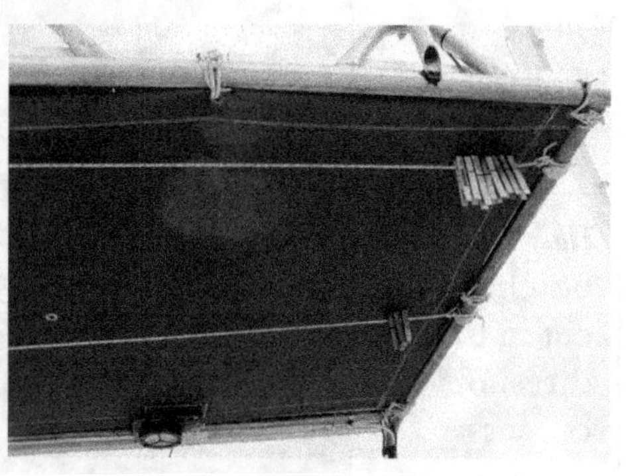

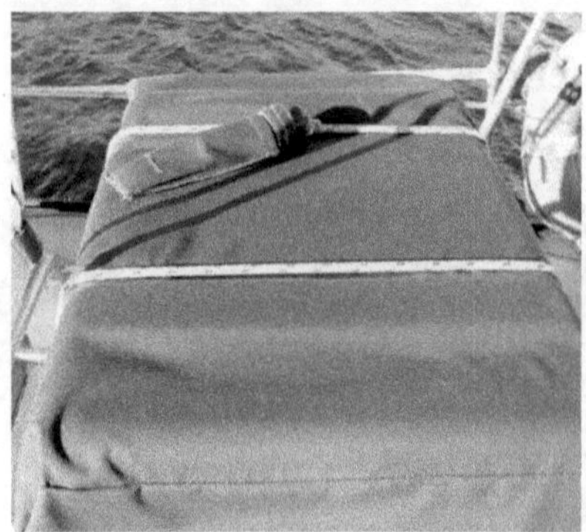

A deck knife handy in its sheath is ready to grab.

This one is tied to the life raft.

Dangerous goods are kept in a self draining deck box.

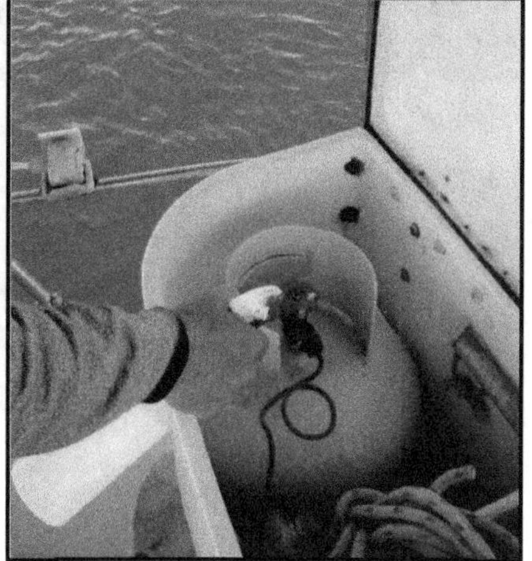

Contents include:

2 gas bottles – Chain and warp for the Danforth – Petrol for the outboard – Fishing gaff and boathook – Odd bits of line needed quickly –The power outlet for the Auto pilot.

Testing the gas bottle with soapy liquid from a spray container kept in the deck box.

The Danforth slides easily into this heavy duty plastic water pipe. Attached to stainless steel stanchion by lashings and SS hose clamps (2).

Catch A Fish

The trolling lure ready to catch a fish in The Recherché Archipelago.

A solid rubber Ocy strap can be used.

It attaches to the tower using braided cord which is continuous with the main line.

A 1 m length of shock cord is tied in a catenary looped into the main line which absorbs the shock when a fish strikes the lure. This prevents the monofilament breaking and loss of gear.

When we sailed as the 4J's and were down below doing lessons we'd have a 2 kg milk can rigged so that when a fish struck, the can fell and hit the deck. The strike unclipped a clothes peg.

Self Steering

The Wind Vane

The Aries wind vane attaches to the emergency tiller.

The block of wood at the base of the deck box seen left is one of two positions for the auto-pilot. This position attaches it directly to the emergency tiller for use in calm conditions.

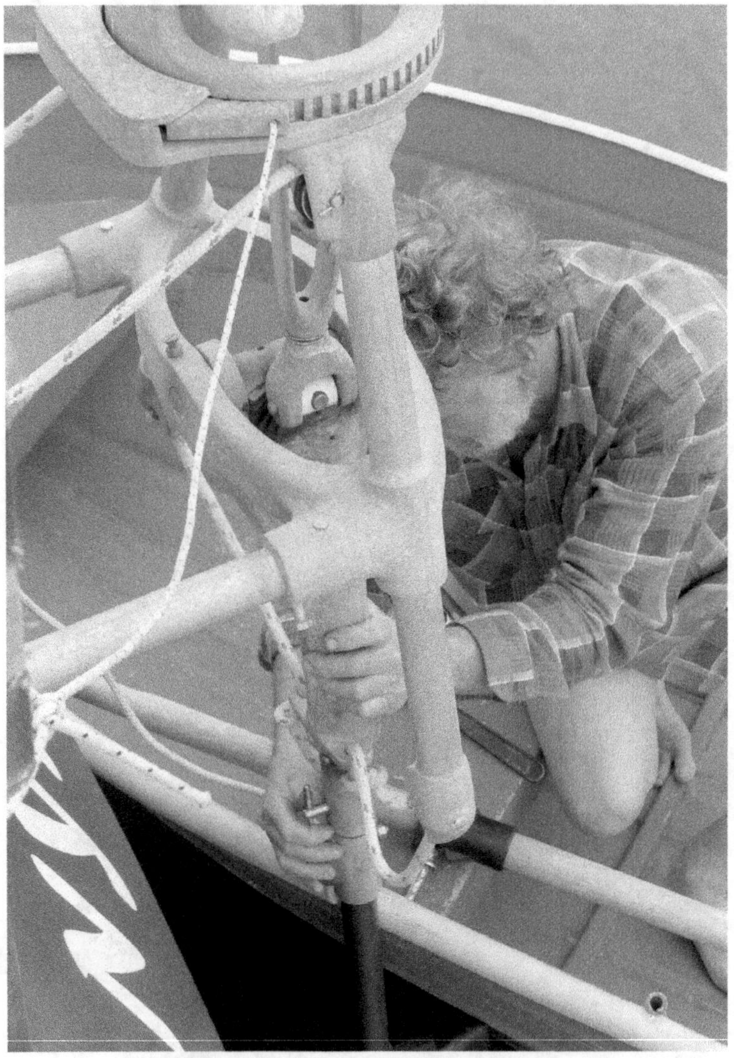

Jack checks and oils the Aries before every passage.

The rope is continuous and occasionally moved along a few inches to increase its life - friction through blocks causes chafe.

> ***Tip.*** Make sure you have lots of spare bushes and bits to suit your device. Mr. Aries is definitely the third man on this ship.

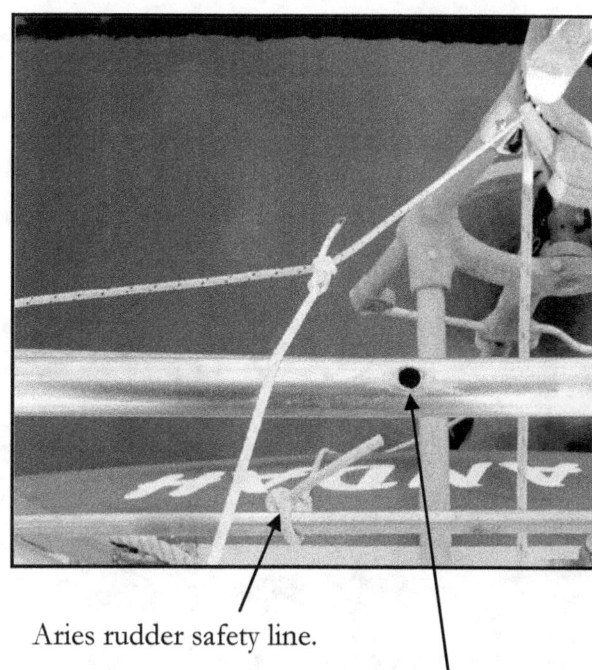

A braided non stretching line is attached to the Aries adjustment line and leads forward to near the cockpit when we are sailing heavy weather.

We are saved many a wetting.

Aries rudder safety line.

Hole in railing for the auto-pilot.

In heavy weather;

The Aries control line in easy reach of the cockpit.

The Auto-Pilot

is used only when motoring in light wind conditions. It attaches to a short dummy vane blade with a pivot point (not shown).

The power connection is inside the deck locker.

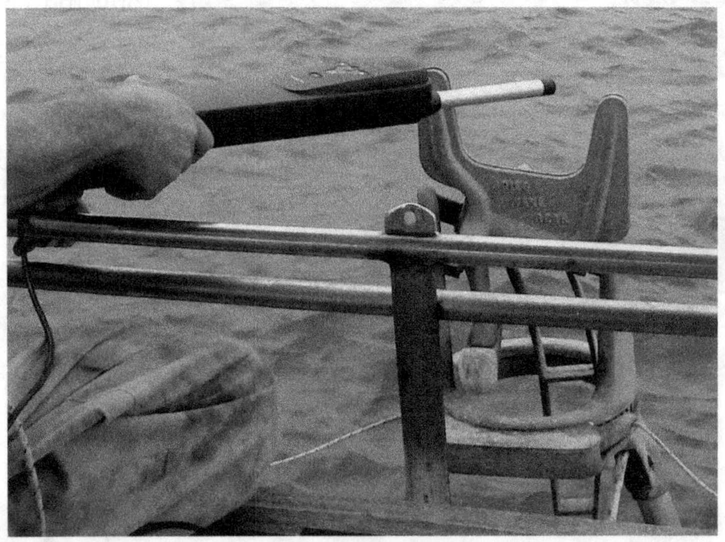

A second position for the auto-pilot in calm conditions attaches it directly to the emergency tiller – It sits on a wooden block at the base of the deck locker.

Before the Mast

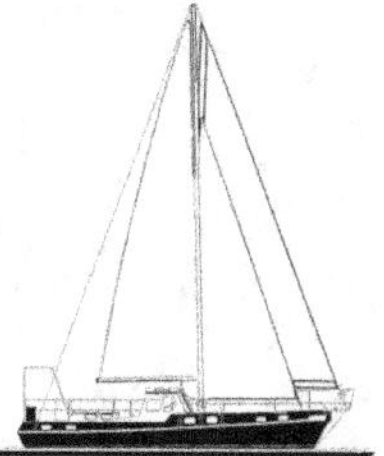

Lots of room to move on the flush deck. Solid rails add security.

The dinghy stows to starboard and the sun awning to port.

The deck hatch under the dinghy can still be opened.

Occasional water coming on board is blocked from rushing below.

Small maintenance jobs can be done at sea. Get rid of those pin barnacles Jack. That's a task not possible if your dinghy is stowed in davits.

Dinghy painter ties to a stanchion.

The dinghy packed for an ocean passage; with fresh water, flares, emergency rations, first aid and fishing gear. When anchored, Jack and I can launch our 10 foot dinghy in less than a minute.

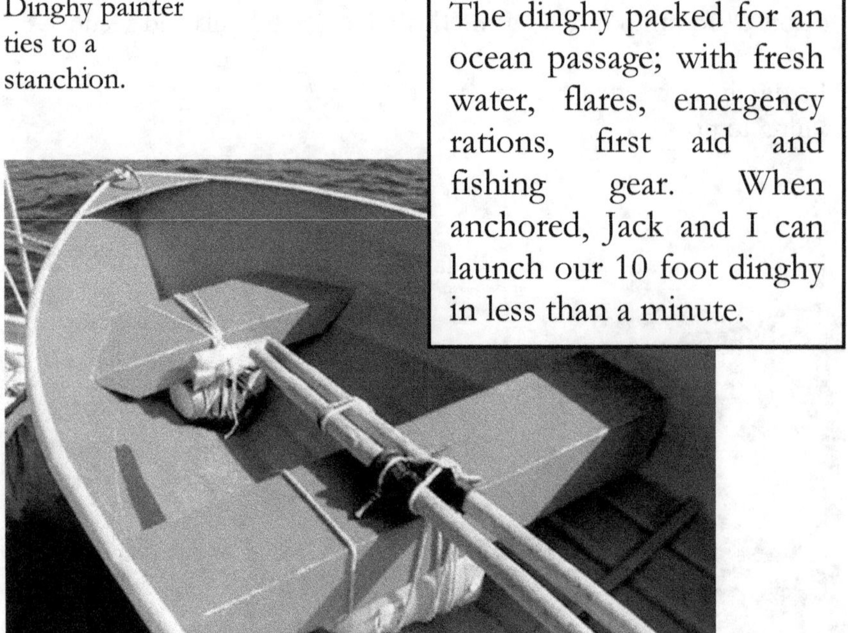

Rigging

Jack checks the rigging before a passage.

Tip. Don't forget the running rigging – end for end sheets spreads chafe and increases their life.

The Bowsprit

Keeps the anchor away from the hull.

The bowsprit makes it easier to clear away ribbon weed which can be a pest.

The twist in the chain is the result of it dragging across a weedy bottom when the boat swings with the wind and current.

Tip. Check the anchor every so often in these conditions, either from the dinghy or by pulling up a few metres of chain.

The Well!

Safety line to deck lid

Yuk!

It's a worthwhile exercise cleaning out the anchor well. We can't risk ribbon weed choking up the hawser pipe and stop the chain running out freely. That's not a position you want to be in.

A good size well is worthwhile. We can easily see how much chain we've let out.

Ground Tackle

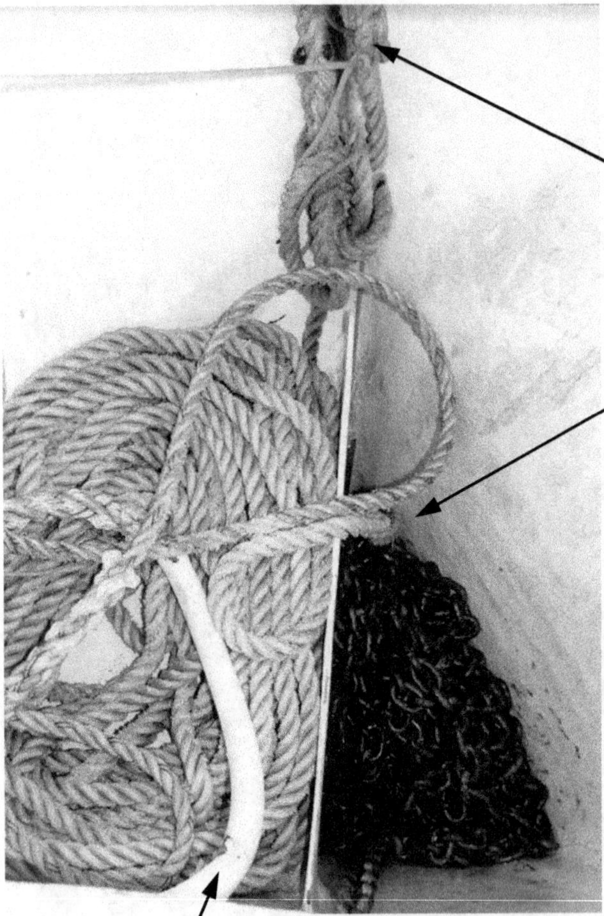

Bitter end of rope tied to the boat.

Anchor rope is spliced to anchor chain.

70 m of 10 mm short link chain on lower level.

100 m of silver rope on upper self draining shelf with built in fiddle.

This keeps the rope from being constantly wet.

The anchor well is self draining.

The 5 m long Nylon Spring that we use when anchoring on chain.

One end has a SS chain grab hook - the other end has plastic water hose to prevent possible chafe over the bow roller and a soft spliced eye that slips over the bollard – there's no way it can jump off.

Anchors

It is essential to have good reliable ground tackle

Everyone has their own favourite anchor. Our main anchor is a 45 lb CQR, a plough type anchor which we've used constantly since we first started sailing *Banyandah* in 1973. The CQR has been a reliable multi bottom anchor and is good for a high impact load such as when used in coral.

We also have a 22 lb Danforth and a heavy Fisherman. As we did not have an anchor winch when we first started sailing, the Danforth was a useful 'lunchtime hook'. When our sons became old enough to be left on board on their own for short periods, we felt comfortable. They were well drilled in what to do in an emergency and between them could lift the Danforth out the holding pipe and lower it overboard if they thought the boat was dragging. The ground tackle was already hooked up. They did this once. An earlier picture shows the Danforth stowed on the aft rail. The Danforth for its weight is extremely good in mud.

All those years the Fisherman, which stows under the cabin sole, was hardly used. When deployed it was never reliable. The flukes were too blunt.

Only the past few years we have tried it when encountering more sea-grass and ribbon weed – Western Australia, S. Australia and southern parts of Australia. We thought it should be a good sea-grass, ribbon-weed anchor. But it was not.

Not until Jack cut away its blunt tips and welded on wider flukes made from 5 mm stainless steel plate.

We were thrilled; first time down it grabbed hold so quick we thought we'd ripped the bow out. Since then it has not failed in wind or swell. We've swum down to it and found it well dug in.

Unfortunately it is difficult to deploy, retrieve and stow because of its bulk and shape.

The Admiralty or Fisherman

The Fisherman Anchor after the addition of two large stainless steel flukes.

What a beauty!

The Fisherman with tips cut off and stainless steel flukes welded on.

The points are really sharp and dig in well.

Glad we didn't jettison this one years ago.

It was picked up for five bucks from the ship breakers when we were building *Banyandah*.

It was made on my birth date – 4/1945.

Tip. When something doesn't work,
you've nothing to lose by trying something to make it work.
These alterations made our fisherman a gem.

The CQR got a face lift and so did I, nearly, when adding lead

Tip. If you pour hot metal, make sure there is no moisture lurking.

Up the Mast

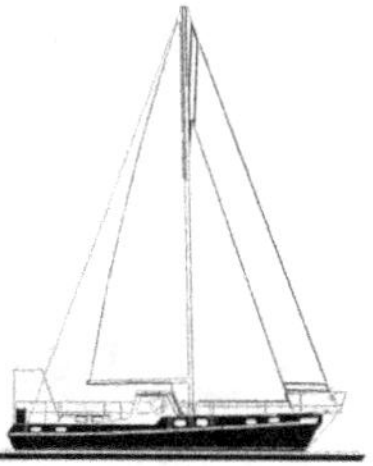

Aboy Wind Sock

The wind sock, made from heavy sail cloth and a few pieces of wire is easily seen from the deck even on a starry night. It is about 250 mm long and swings on a rod attached to the aft side of the mast.

The LED deck lights are brilliant on dark nights.
1 up and 2 down.

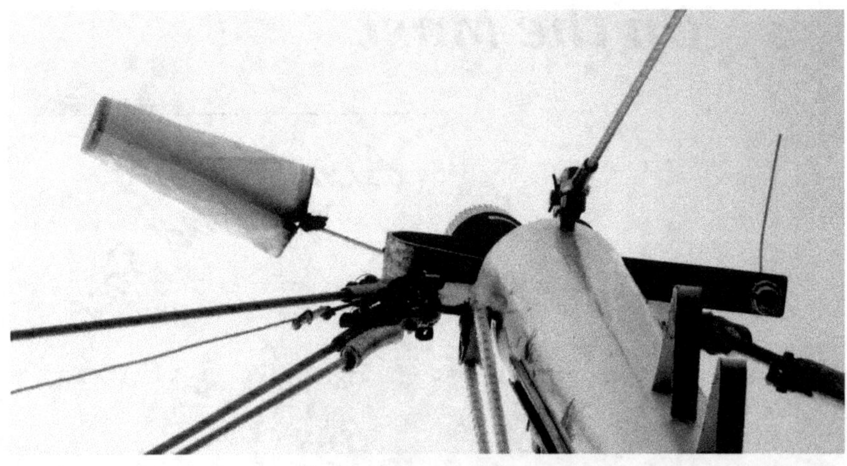

When bringing up the anchor a quick look at the windsock helps me keep Miss B in line with the action and the wind.

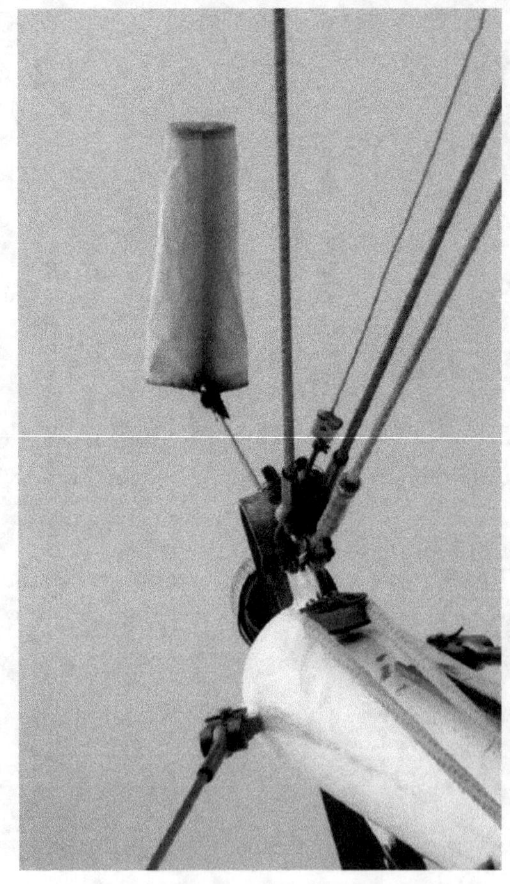

What you need to make a Wind Sock..

1 m stainless steel fishing wire trace. About 250 mm of 5 mm stainless rod threaded one end with nut to suit and thick washer that will snugly slide on. The washer supports the wind sock and is firmly set in place with Sikiflex underneath only – otherwise the sock won't turn freely.

Shape a cone out of sailcloth so it will end up being about 250 mm finished length. Don't forget to leave enough material to hem the smaller end and sew around the wire circle at larger end. It can always be cut shorter from one end if you make it too long.

The windsock was robust enough to withstand twin ospreys having fun. We were anchored at the homestead on Dirk Hartog Island, Shark Bay, WA.

This stick nest was possibly the one sketched by the Freycinet expedition in 1818.

How To Make A Wind Sock

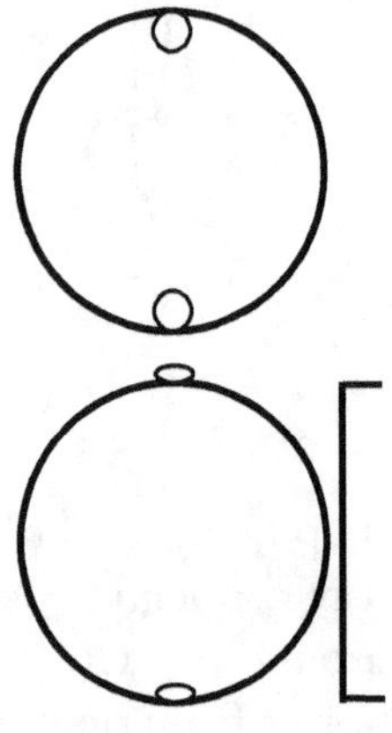

1/ Form a circle with the wire trace to make a 100-110 mm diameter ring, shaping little rings in line with each other as you go. Jack shapes these little rings round a pencil. Continue on with a second round of wire inter-twining it with the first. Depending on the wire thickness, once for the little rings 'might' be sufficient to work well on the rod. But still go at least twice around the main ring to give stiffness.

2/ Bend the little rings 90° to the big ring, both the same side. Align and test on the rod to make sure it swings freely.

3/ Cut the sailcloth to form a cone when stitched to fit the main wire ring, tapering it to a 60 mm diameter opening at the trailing edge. Form a 10 mm hem on trailing edge and sew, then seam the cone's length leaving about 15 mm open at large end. Turn inside out so edges are inside. Keep seam at bottom.

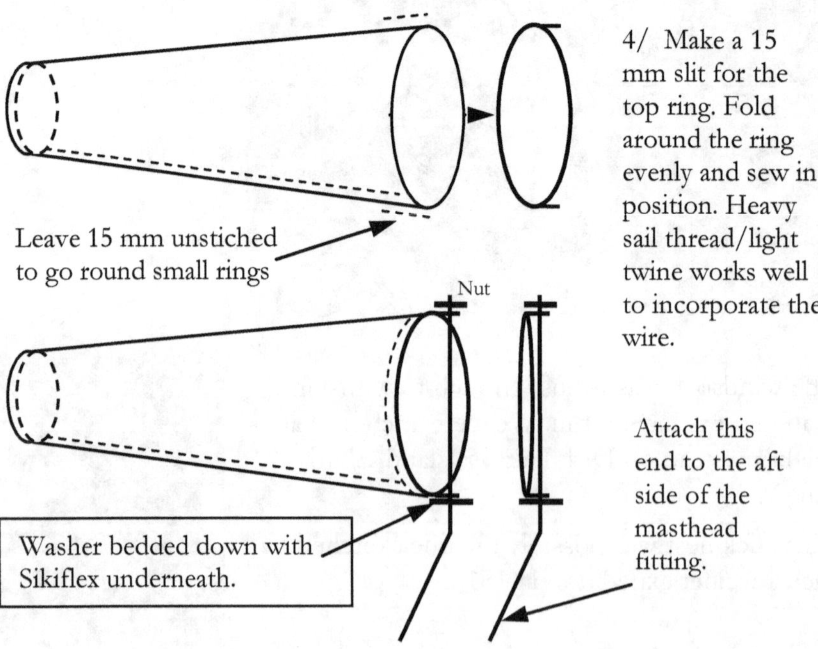

4/ Make a 15 mm slit for the top ring. Fold around the ring evenly and sew in position. Heavy sail thread/light twine works well to incorporate the wire.

Sun Awning/ Rain Catcher

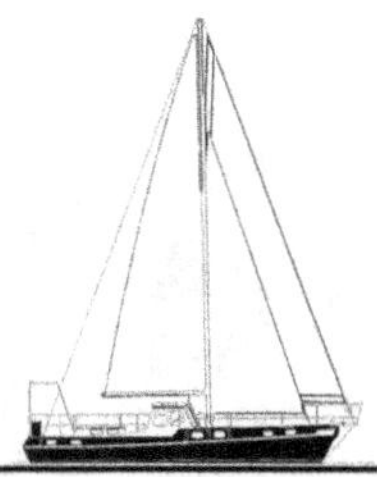

Attached aft to the tower, the sun awning shades more than half of the boat.

It is a simple light weight structure that is easy to erect and take down even in windy conditions.

A few lines each side prevent it billowing in the wind and controls the collection or discharge of rain water.

A piece of old dinghy mast spreads the awning so it doesn't sag.

The awning rolls up on that tube from front to back and stows out of the way on the foredeck.

The rip-stop Vinyl is heat seamed down the centreline to extend the cloth width.

A silver rope tensioning line each side forms a lip to stop run off when used as a rain catcher. The fore and aft outer edges of the awning have been cut slightly concave to assist – causing the edges to curl slightly and catch the rain.

> ***Tip.*** If you make the awning yourself and need wider material than you can buy – it is worth having the seam heat sealed. Most places that sell the material can do this.
>
> This avoids leakage down the center of the boat and doubles the material where it touches the sail or boom.

The side ropes pull forward and are tensioned on the cap shrouds.

This is the last thing done when unrolling the awning forward.

It is first placed on the main boom just forward of the topping lift and fixed to the tower.

Small side lines hold it down to the hand railing.

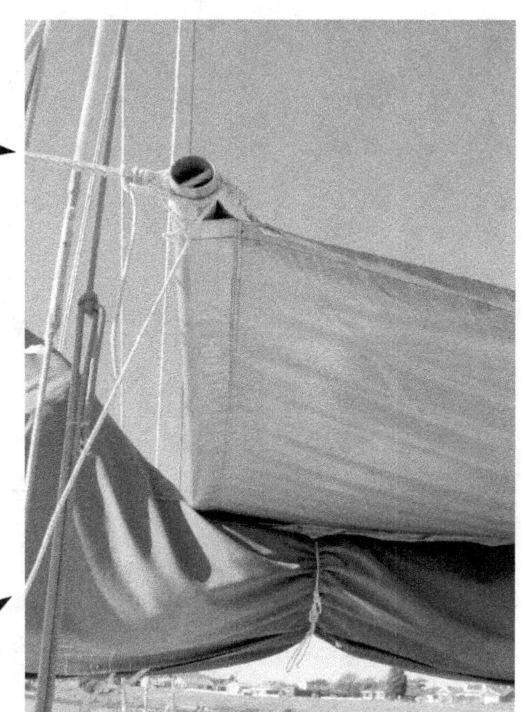

The two stays sometime chatter if the wind is strong. This is when we use a noodle.

Tip. Sew a wear pad on the sail cover where the awning rests when it is up. It is easier to replace that than the sail cover.

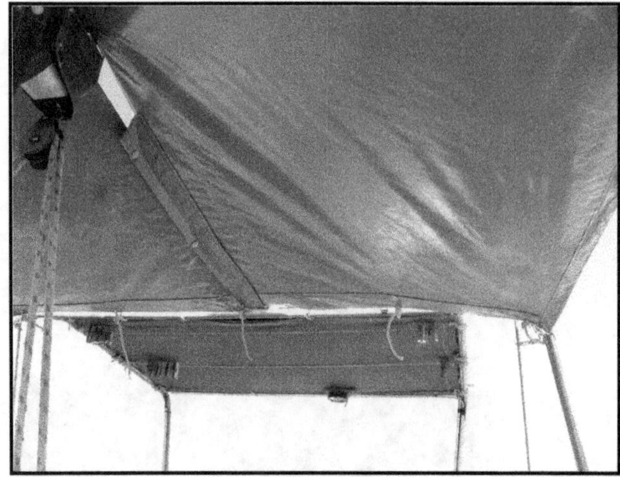

To allow for the topping lift, the awning splits in two and comes together again with the use of plastic toggles.

A piece of webbing sewn on prevents wear against the topping lift.

Top view of the awning attached to the tower

Fastening the awning to the tower

Pieces of silver rope with a spliced loop are passed through an eyelet in the awning then a figure of eight knot is tied. Once the rope has passed around the tower, the knot goes through the loop. They don't come undone when the awning is under tension.

They make very cheap fastenings.

Apart from the main pole this clip that fastens to the backstay is the only piece of metal hardware.

On windy days there is little chance of being hit in the eye.

Cheap hardware

Catching Rain Water

The hoses are in place directly above the deck fillers.

Tip. Fuel and Water Deck Fittings should not look alike to help prevent accidental mix-ups.

So Simple

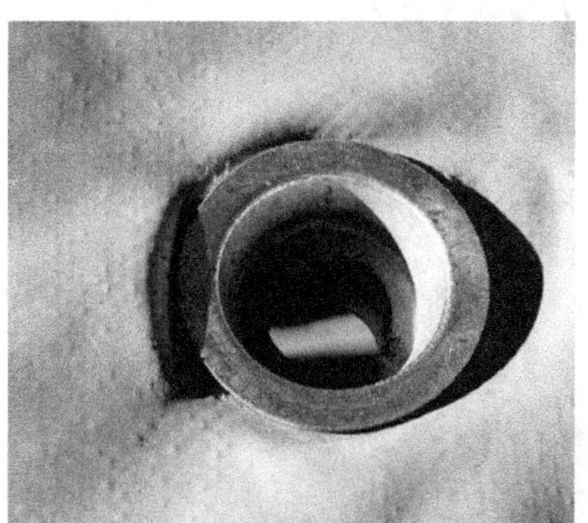

A caravan sink drain does the trick.

Punch a hole in the vinyl and then screw it on.

Just push on the hose.

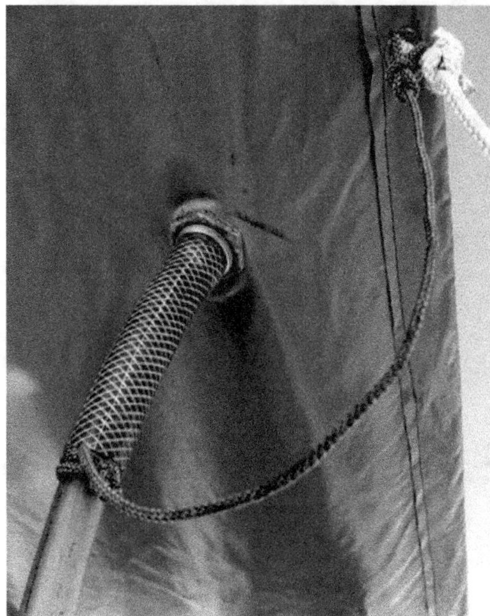

Attach the safety line so the hose won't fall overboard.

Tip. When you don't want to catch rainwater, tensioning the side line to the handrail allows all rainwater to go straight over the side it.

Running The Boat/ and Other Bits

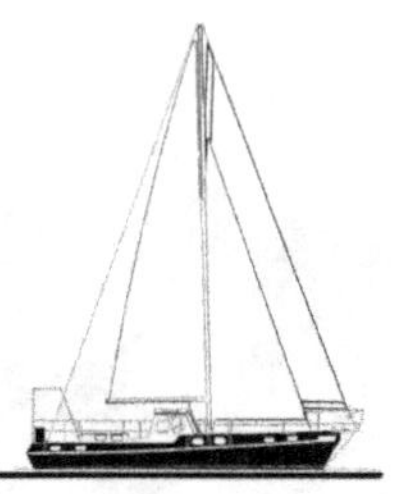

Steps up the mast

The Spinnaker Poles are permanently lashed to rings on the front of the mast. They have their own topping lifts for lowering into position or pulling up to store against the mast when not in use.

Running Back Stays

Perfect when in heavy weather with the staysail set.

Made using SPECTRA to minimize stretch, and very good blocks.

They store well, one each side of the boat, against the aft lower shrouds.

Assembly is quick. We run it aft – it attaches to a permanent shackle on an aft chain plate and snap it on.

When I look up through the head's deck hatch, it is so good to see the mast not doing a jig.

Quality snap shackle and multi-fall block and tackle for tensioning.

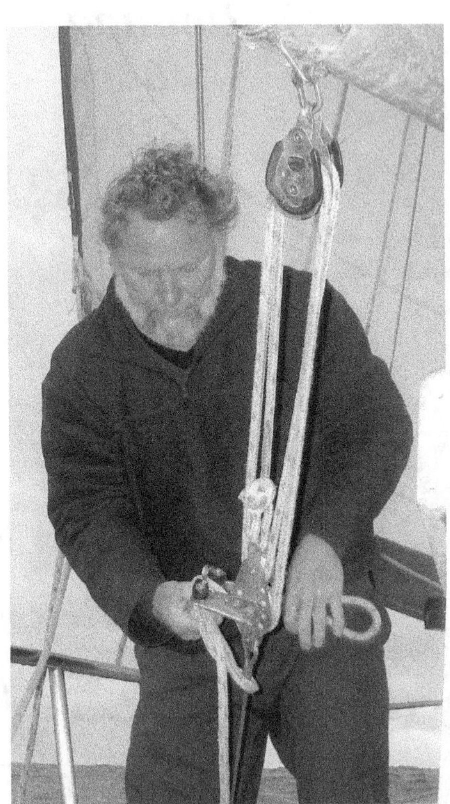

DON'T ACCIDENTLY JIBE

Jack restraining the boom with a preventer.

It doubles as a downhaul.

A half-hitch after jamming the sheet prevents accidental release and is quickly undone.

The vang gets used all the time on *Banyandah* to prevent accidents and broken gear.

The boom restrained.

CHECKING CHAFE CHECK MATE

The person on watch has that responsibility.

Chafe'. To wear away or irritate by rubbing. Not good. A very irritating problem.

Chafe can ruin ropes quickly. Check sheets frequently for chafe. At night check with a torch.

If one should chafe through it's a nightmare. A perfectly good sail can be ruined in the time it takes to get it down.

End for end sheets to move the wear position.

You are more likely to hear blocks squeak when lying in your bunk – well then, there's something amiss – a block about to break? – a rope chafing?

Tip. Using a sewing awl is a quick way to sew on chafe pads.

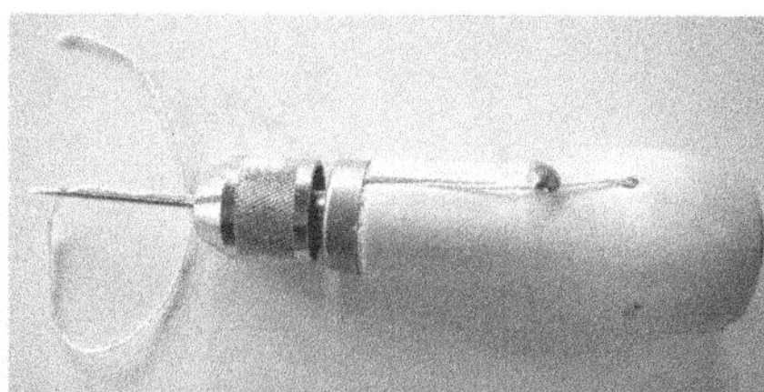

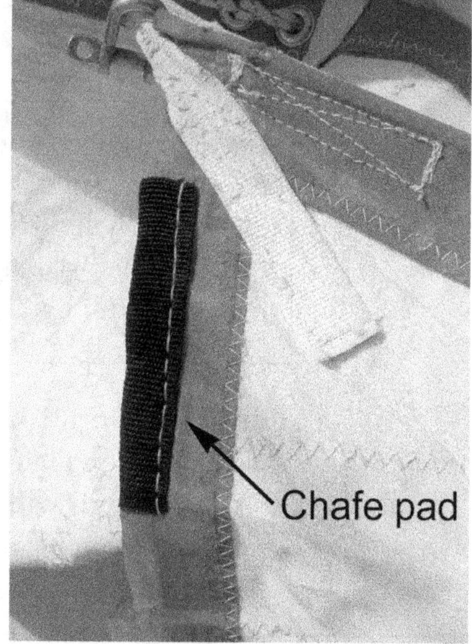

Tip. Allow extra length on sheets. A sheet can be shortened to bring another part of the rope into play say through a block by using a larger bowline at the clew or leaving a longer tail.

A stitch in time saves nine, and perhaps a blown out sail.

Worn stitching being replaced on the head of the mainsail.

Standing on the hard dodger top I don't have to take the sail down.

Instead of a sailors palm I stick a piece of masking tape to the concave surface of a teaspoon. I press the needle through the hole with my thumb on the backside of the spoon. The needle does not slip.

> ***Tip.*** Use a very short hand sewing needle with a big eye. It will pass through the original stitch holes and not break.

The sail motif that was on all *Banyandah's* sails when we sailed as a family – All our initials start with a J.

Black stick on sail tape.

> ***Tip.*** A length of rubber water hose split lengthways can be quickly snapped onto a sheet to stop chafe where it touches the railing.

Plastic Pipe around Stays to prevent chafe

Our young son well wedged in between the stays and the solid safety railing. Quite secure.

Rigid plastic PVC tubing around the stay of *Banyandah's* original galvanized rigging when she was ketch rigged.

Anti-chafe for the sails. They slide smoothly around the stays.

We use polyethylene tubing round *Banyandah's* new stainless rig.

Moorings

We used this mooring in the Abrolhos in Western Australia. It was clearly marked with the size vessel it suited and was checked annually.

Not all moorings are like this one. None should be trusted – that would be foolhardy.

Don't chance that it will hold your boat.

Test it with a good steady pull.

Many a fisherman has loaned us their mooring. They generally have chunky ones with big size chain. Down south they often bring the chain to a big hook on their bow.

If we use a fisherman's mooring set up that way we pull the chain to the bow then slip our own warp through a link and bring both ends, one is usually a soft loop, to the bollard.

By doing this we are hanging on our own line and can simply let the mooring go by slipping our line.

Tip. Professional fishers are a wealth of local knowledge. Most are more than happy to share this.

Blocks

Don't forget the blocks.

Grit and dirt blown from shore will abrade the smooth running of blocks.

Flat spots can occur causing problems with the smooth operating of halyards or sheets controlling roller-furlers.

Every now and again all blocks should be washed and lightly oil. WD-40 only good for a quick fix.

Tip. Squirt blocks with freshwater when you're alongside.

Their life will be longer.

This block has just recently disintegrated. It was one of the original blocks on *Banyandah* from 1973 and has sailed many thousands of miles.

The Sail Track

Sail tracks should also be washed down. Once a year from the top of the mast if you can.

Before a long passage Jack will climb the mast and spray the sail track with silicon so there's no unexpected trouble when it comes to reefing. He is especially careful when he does this that he doesn't get any silicon on our mast steps. Silicon makes everything it comes in contact with very slippery indeed.

Tip. Spray silicon on a calm day. Avoid where it's not meant to be slippery.

Watch Keepers Safety Belt

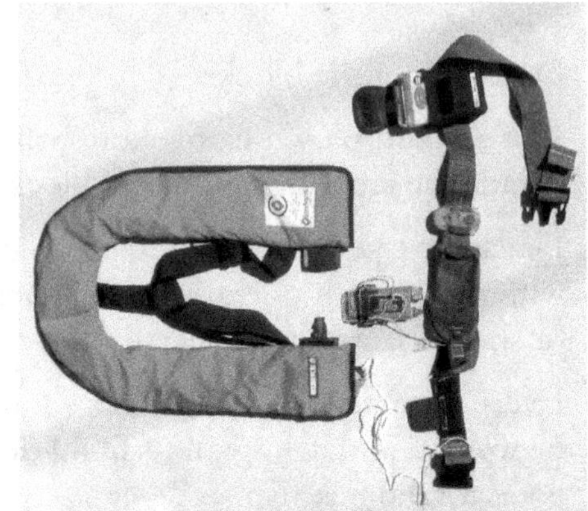

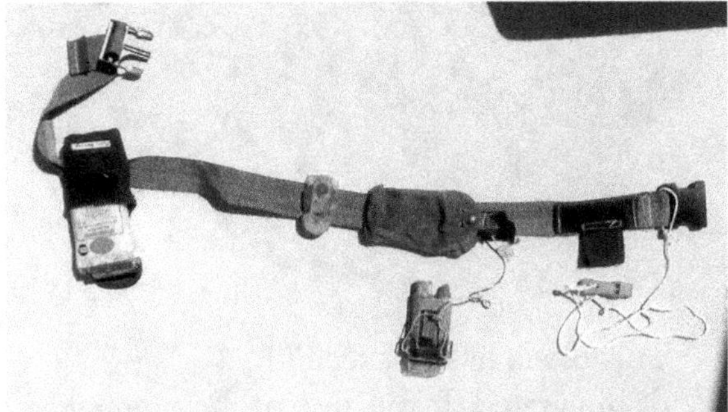

Pea-less whistle slips into a tiny pocket.

Mobilert transponder sounds alarm when MOB

High Powered Strobe

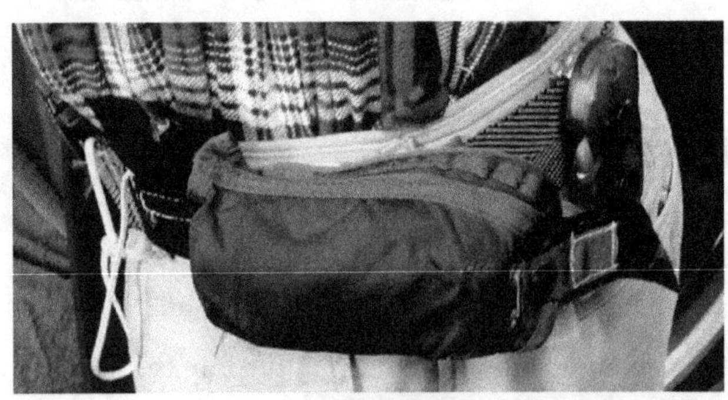

PLB Personal Location Beacon

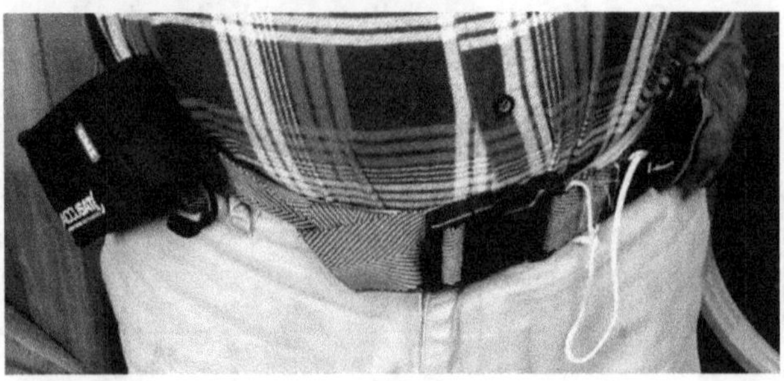

The Ship's Log

We keep a log of our journey. We record cumulative miles *Banyandah* has run, course steered, miles achieved, wind speed and direction, barometric pressure, plus any notes we like to make. Sound like a chore? Not a bit. In fact, when the ship's bell strikes the hour we relish the opportunity to record our passage.

More than 35 years ago we started with store bought log books, which proved too expensive, so we soon designed our own and had the pages Xeroxed and put in a manila folder. In Sri Lanka for just a few dollars we had a 300 page volume printed and bound.

Today we use lined A4 hardback notebooks obtainable from most newsagents for about $5, and rule the columns ourselves.

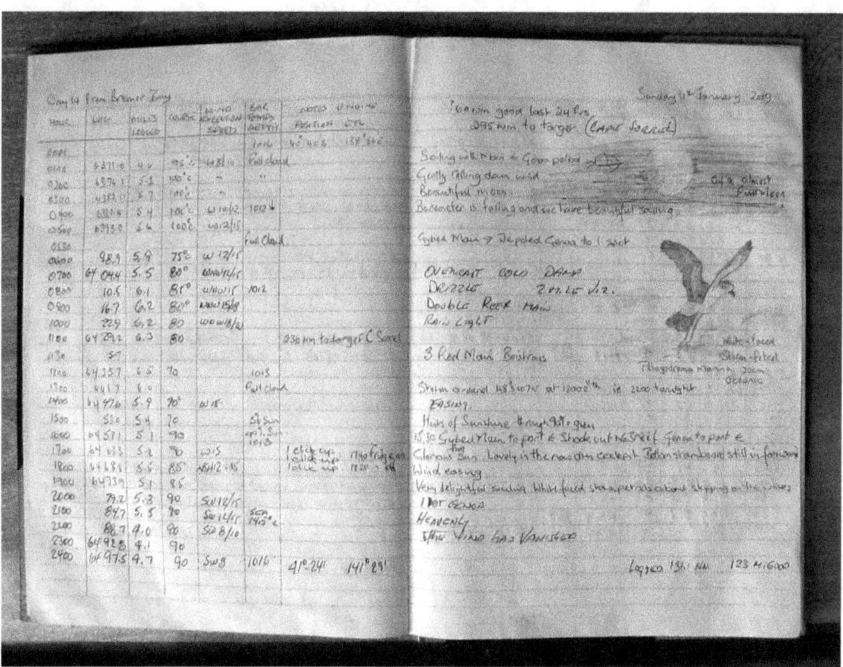

The right hand page is for comments; anything to do with sail changes, whatever we like. We might draw a little boat showing the sail plan with wind arrows, wildlife seen, and the stats.

Day 7 Out from Albany — M.N. 39°37'S 131°40'E

HOUR	LOG	MILES LOGGED	SKY SWELL	COURSE	WIND	BAR TEMPS DEPTH	NOTES ENGINE POSITION etc.
0000	12301	766	3M	80°	SSW40	1013	MAIN DOWN
0	12307	772	cloud		"		Small No 3 Jib only
0100	12307	772	cloud	-80-	"		
0200		778	cloud		"	1014	39°28.95S 132°00.79E
0300	12319	784	2 tiny patches of skies	80	"		
0400	12326	791	cloud	70	SSW30	18.9°ST 1015½	39°25.32S 132°08 48E
0500	12331	796 (bar)	"	70	SSW30/35	17°CT	
0530							
0700	12343	808	CLOUD RAIN	70	SSW 20/30	18.5 ST 1018	39°-18'S 132°28.6E
0800	12349	814	"	70	SSW 25/35	1019	
0900	12355	820	hint of sun	70	SSW25/30		

On this voyage we had a sky and swell column

The column 'Notes – Position, Engine etc is particularly good. In it we record our position from the GPS a few times a day, and whenever important things happen on board; such as when a gas bottle runs out, number of litres of diesel pumped from our main storage tanks into the 'day tank'

Engine oil top ups.

Weather forecasts.

Number of litres of diesel taken on board.

And when we fill our water tanks.

Tip. Make your own logbooks. They'll end up being more informative and treasured than store bought logbooks.

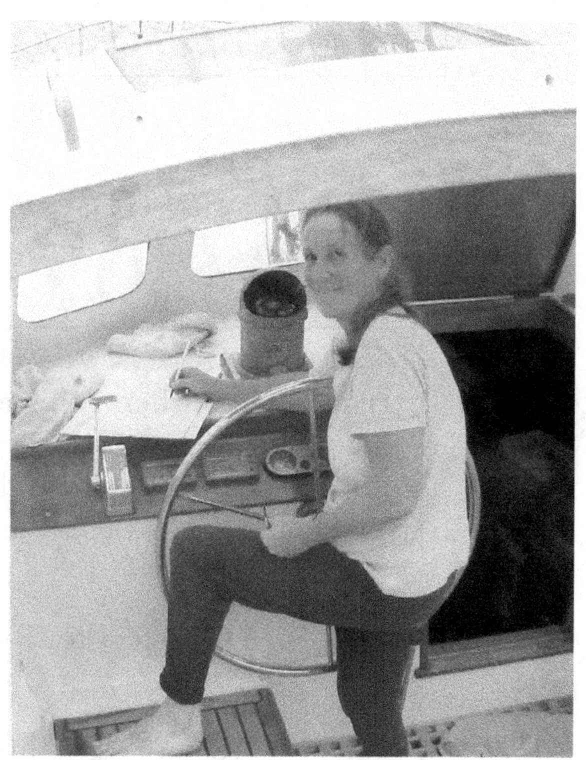

Jude marking the logbook at the end of a day sail.

This takes just a minute.

We now have a wonderful record of comments, some humorous, some laconic, a few distressed.

They form an informative record of a journey we never want to forget.

On a passage we might mark the log every hour.

On a day sail just when we want.

And on non-sailing days, one page of the log book might cover a few days in notes.

Short notes of maintenance done, or needs to be done are also useful.

It's so much easier to check in the log than to have to think back, ummm? Whether something was done or not?

MOST IMPORTANT

The Dinghy Painter

Use floating rope as a dinghy painter. Then when going astern there's no chance it fouling the prop and perhaps stalling the engine in a dangerous situation.

Silver rope is perfect for the job.

Splice an eye in one end just big enough to drop over a stern bollard when stepping on board.

More Pictures

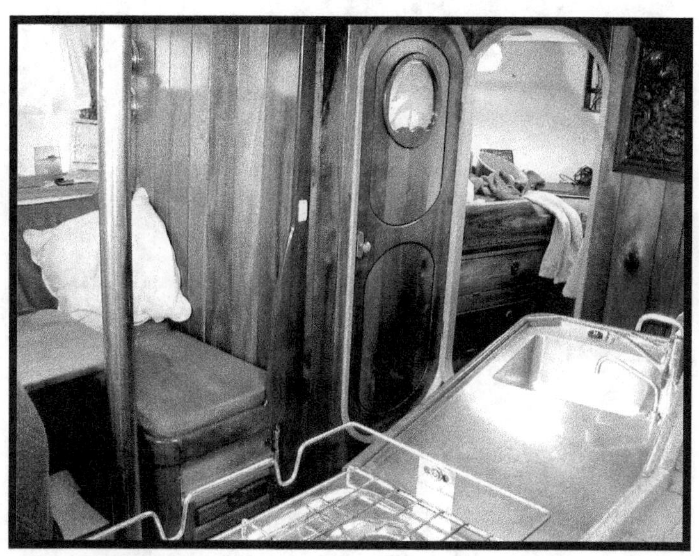

The Solar Light on the tower. Coming home after dark we can always find the boat.

Coming on automatically, it acts as an anchor light and we don't have to worry so much about being rammed in a busy anchorage if we're unexpectedly late from the shore.

At the masthead is our main anchor light.

Hand drawn by Jerome D Binder

Age 13

www.ingramcontent.com/pod-product-compliance
Lightning Source LLC
Chambersburg PA
CBHW050600300426
44112CB00013B/2005

* 9 7 8 0 9 8 0 8 7 2 0 4 0 *